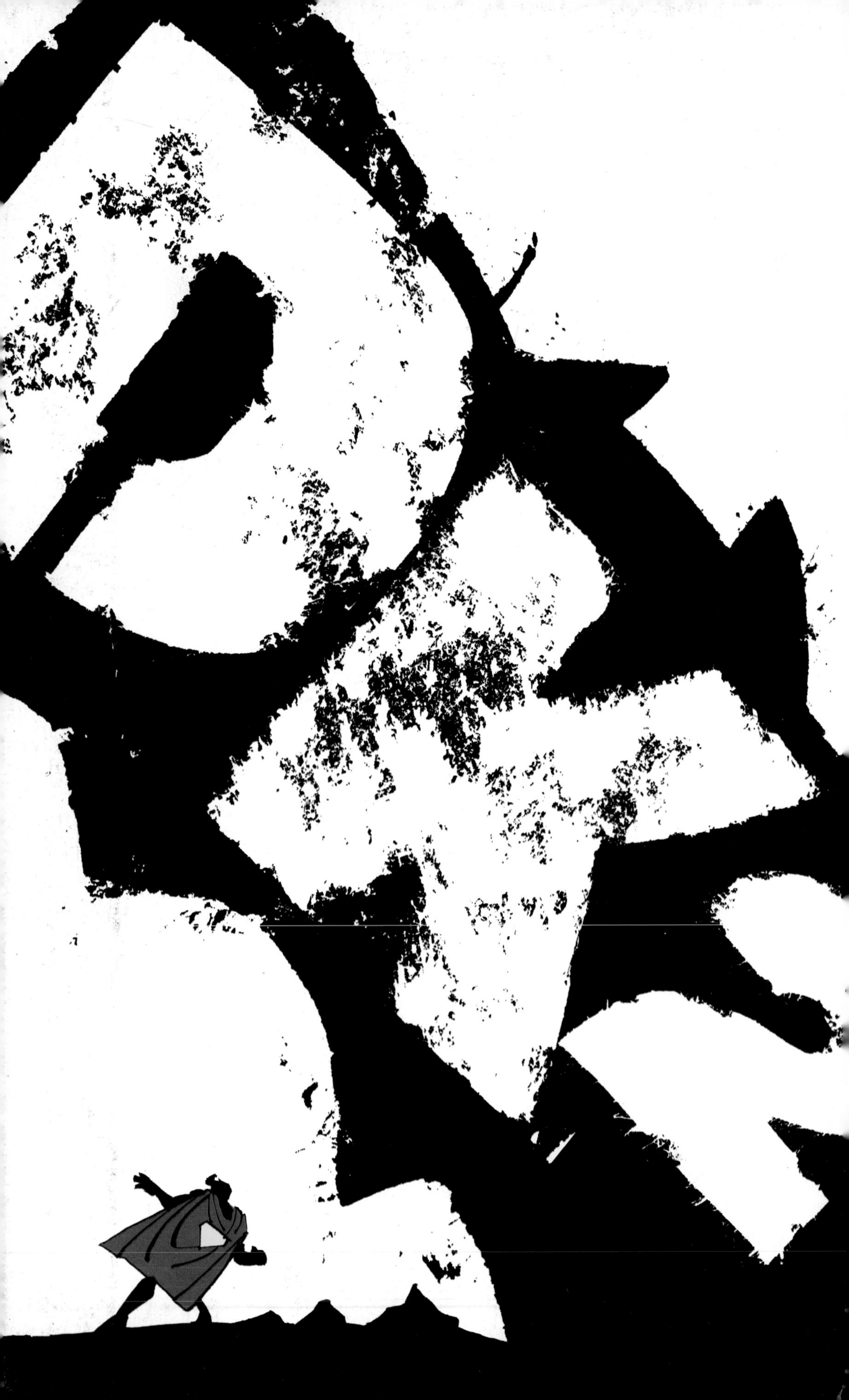

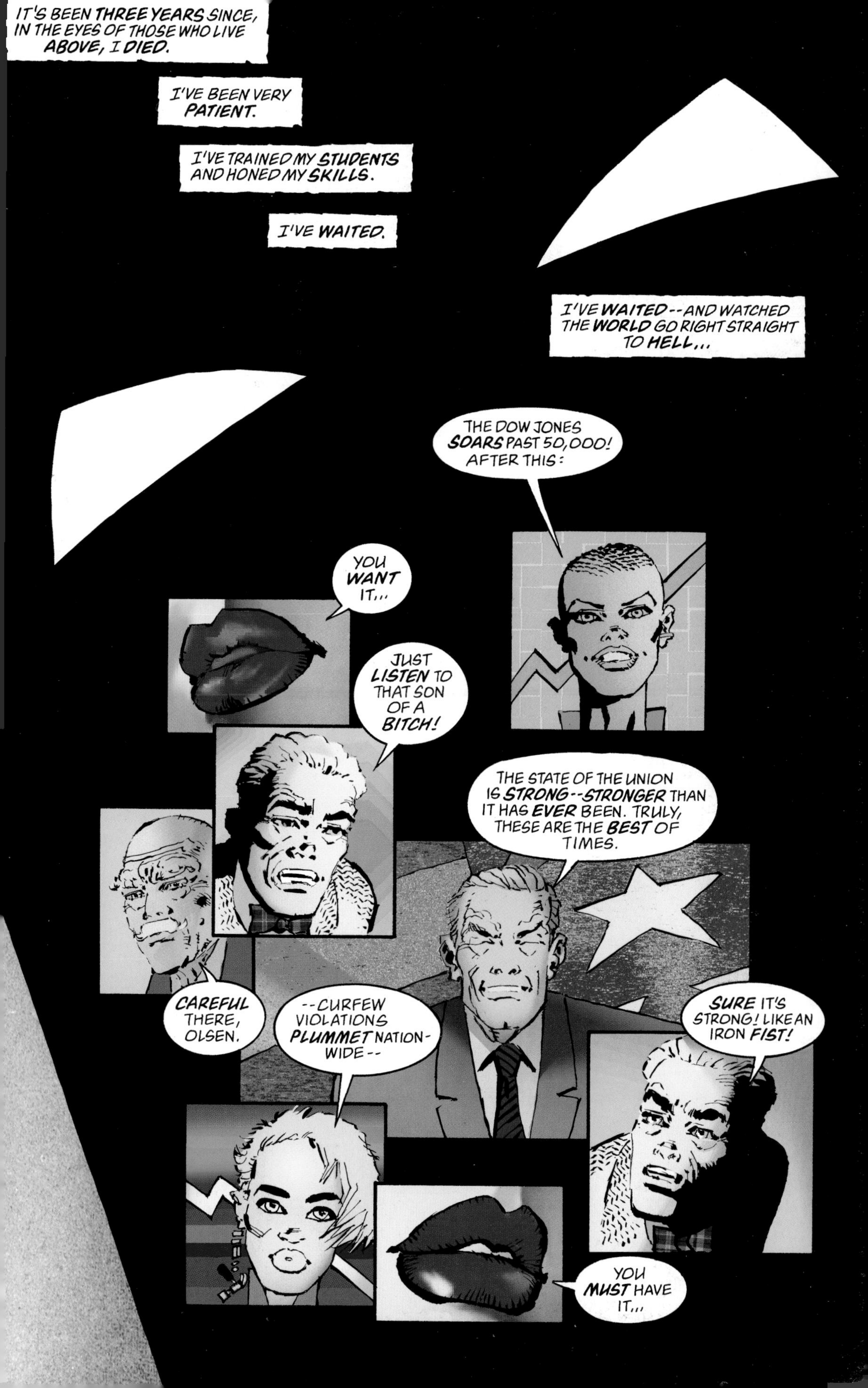
IT'S BEEN THREE YEARS SINCE, IN THE EYES OF THOSE WHO LIVE ABOVE, I DIED.
I'VE BEEN VERY PATIENT.
I'VE TRAINED MY STUDENTS AND HONED MY SKILLS.
I'VE WAITED.
I'VE WAITED--AND WATCHED THE WORLD GO RIGHT STRAIGHT TO HELL...
THE DOW JONES SOARS PAST 50,000! AFTER THIS:
YOU WANT IT...
JUST LISTEN TO THAT SON OF A BITCH!
THE STATE OF THE UNION IS STRONG--STRONGER THAN IT HAS EVER BEEN. TRULY, THESE ARE THE BEST OF TIMES.
CAREFUL THERE, OLSEN.
--CURFEW VIOLATIONS PLUMMET NATION-WIDE--
SURE IT'S STRONG! LIKE AN IRON FIST!
YOU MUST HAVE IT...

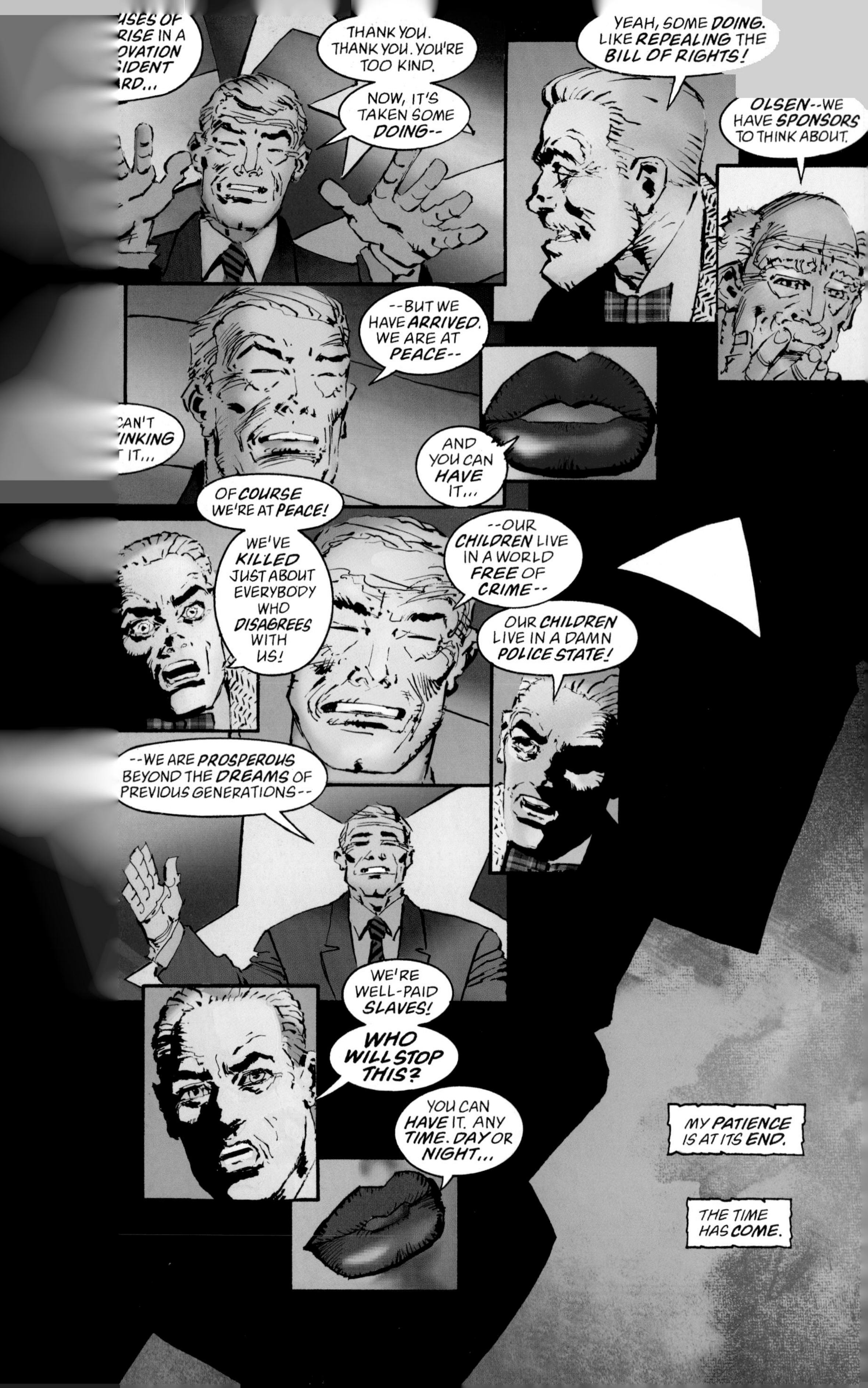
USES OF
RISE IN A
OVATION
SIDENT
ARD...
THANK YOU. THANK YOU. YOU'RE TOO KIND.
NOW, IT'S TAKEN SOME DOING--
YEAH, SOME DOING. LIKE REPEALING THE BILL OF RIGHTS!
OLSEN--WE HAVE SPONSORS TO THINK ABOUT.
--BUT WE HAVE ARRIVED. WE ARE AT PEACE--
CAN'T
INKING
T IT...
AND YOU CAN HAVE IT...
OF COURSE WE'RE AT PEACE!
WE'VE KILLED JUST ABOUT EVERYBODY WHO DISAGREES WITH US!
--OUR CHILDREN LIVE IN A WORLD FREE OF CRIME--
OUR CHILDREN LIVE IN A DAMN POLICE STATE!
--WE ARE PROSPEROUS BEYOND THE DREAMS OF PREVIOUS GENERATIONS--
WE'RE WELL-PAID SLAVES!
WHO WILL STOP THIS?
YOU CAN HAVE IT. ANY TIME. DAY OR NIGHT...
MY PATIENCE IS AT ITS END.
THE TIME HAS COME.

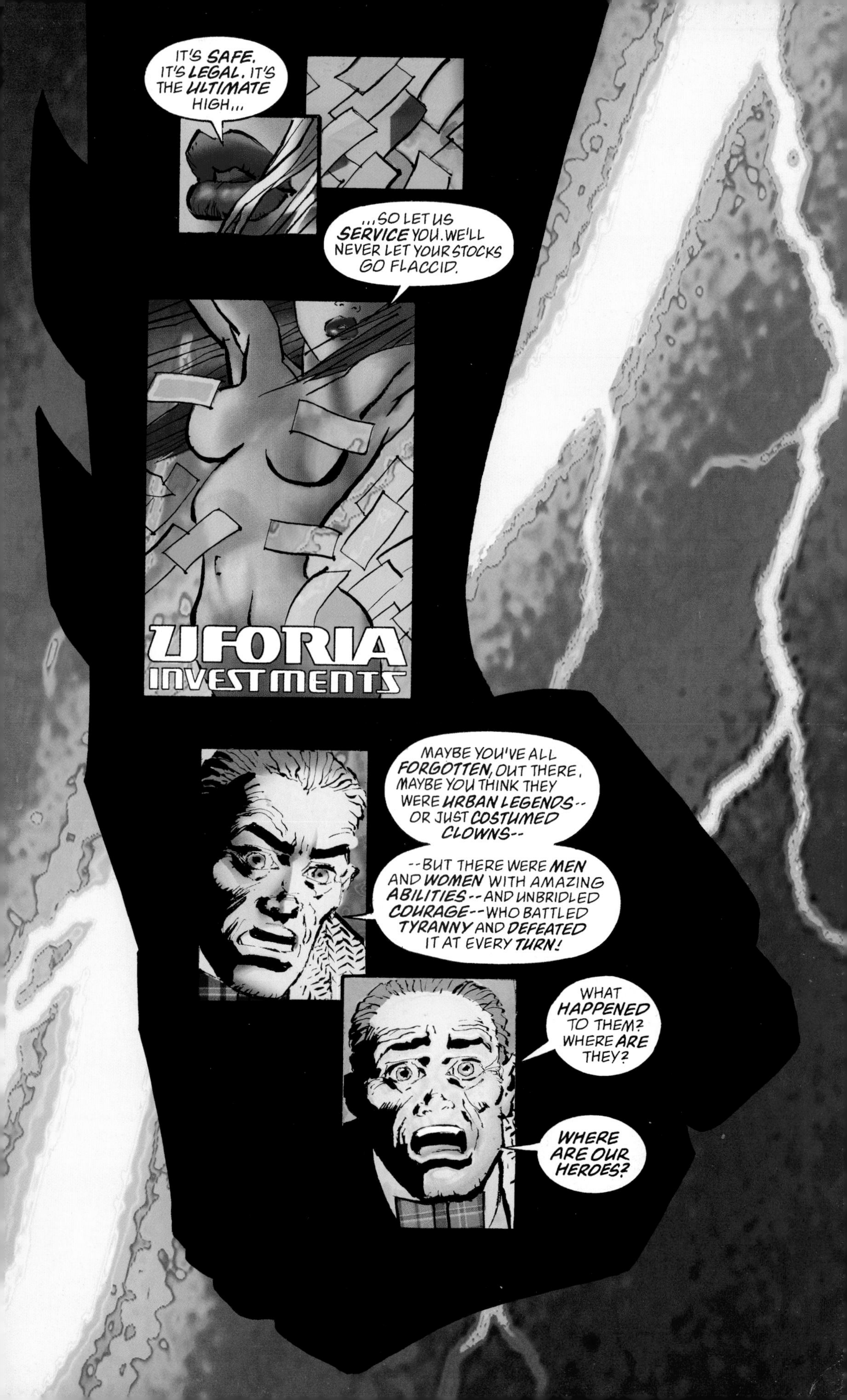

IT'S SAFE. IT'S LEGAL. IT'S THE ULTIMATE HIGH...
...SO LET US SERVICE YOU. WE'LL NEVER LET YOUR STOCKS GO FLACCID.
UFORIA INVESTMENTS
MAYBE YOU'VE ALL FORGOTTEN, OUT THERE. MAYBE YOU THINK THEY WERE URBAN LEGENDS-- OR JUST COSTUMED CLOWNS--
--BUT THERE WERE MEN AND WOMEN WITH AMAZING ABILITIES--AND UNBRIDLED COURAGE--WHO BATTLED TYRANNY AND DEFEATED IT AT EVERY TURN!
WHAT HAPPENED TO THEM? WHERE ARE THEY?
WHERE ARE OUR HEROES?

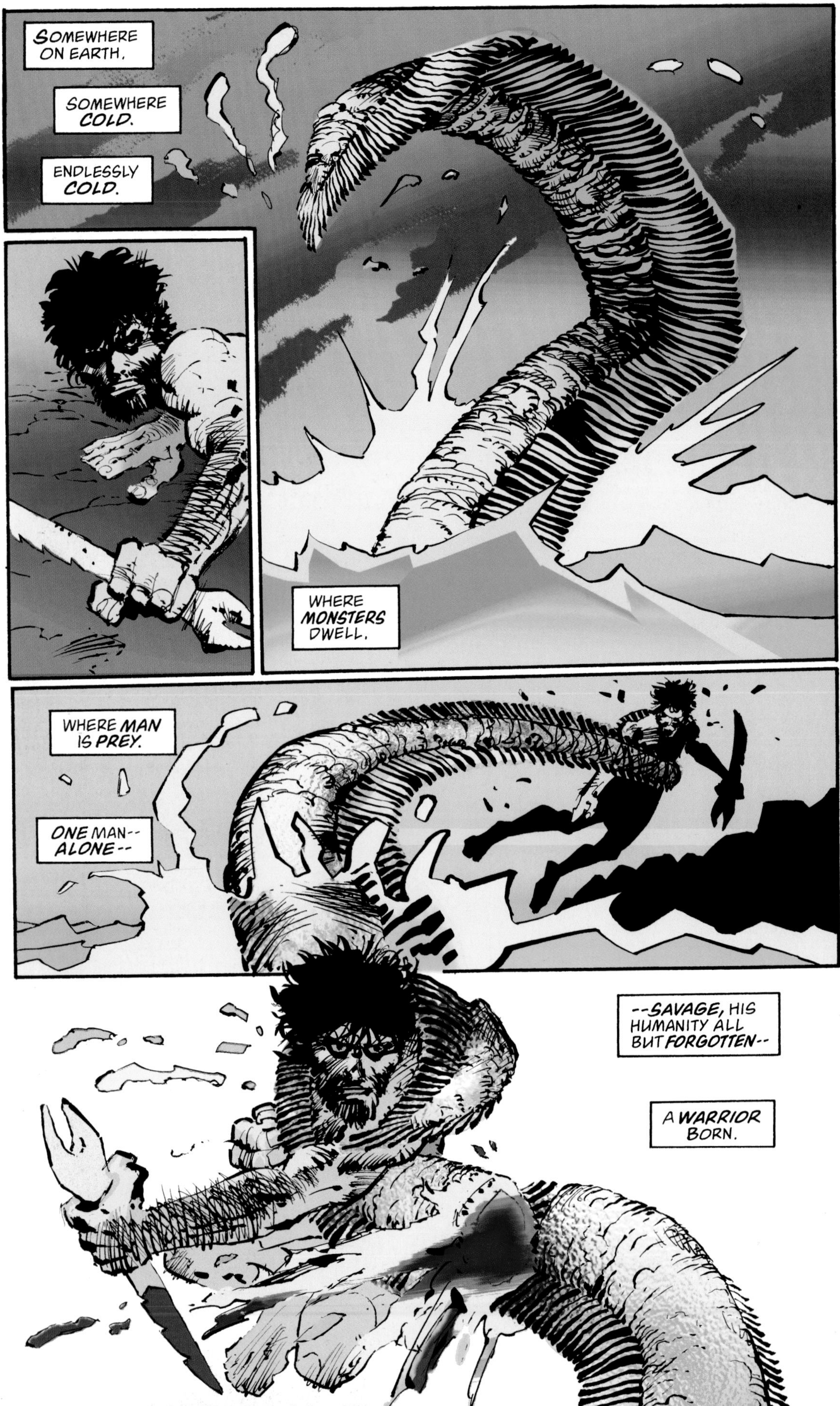
SOMEWHERE ON EARTH.
SOMEWHERE COLD.
ENDLESSLY COLD.
WHERE MONSTERS DWELL.
WHERE MAN IS PREY.
ONE MAN-- ALONE--
--SAVAGE, HIS HUMANITY ALL BUT FORGOTTEN--
A WARRIOR BORN.

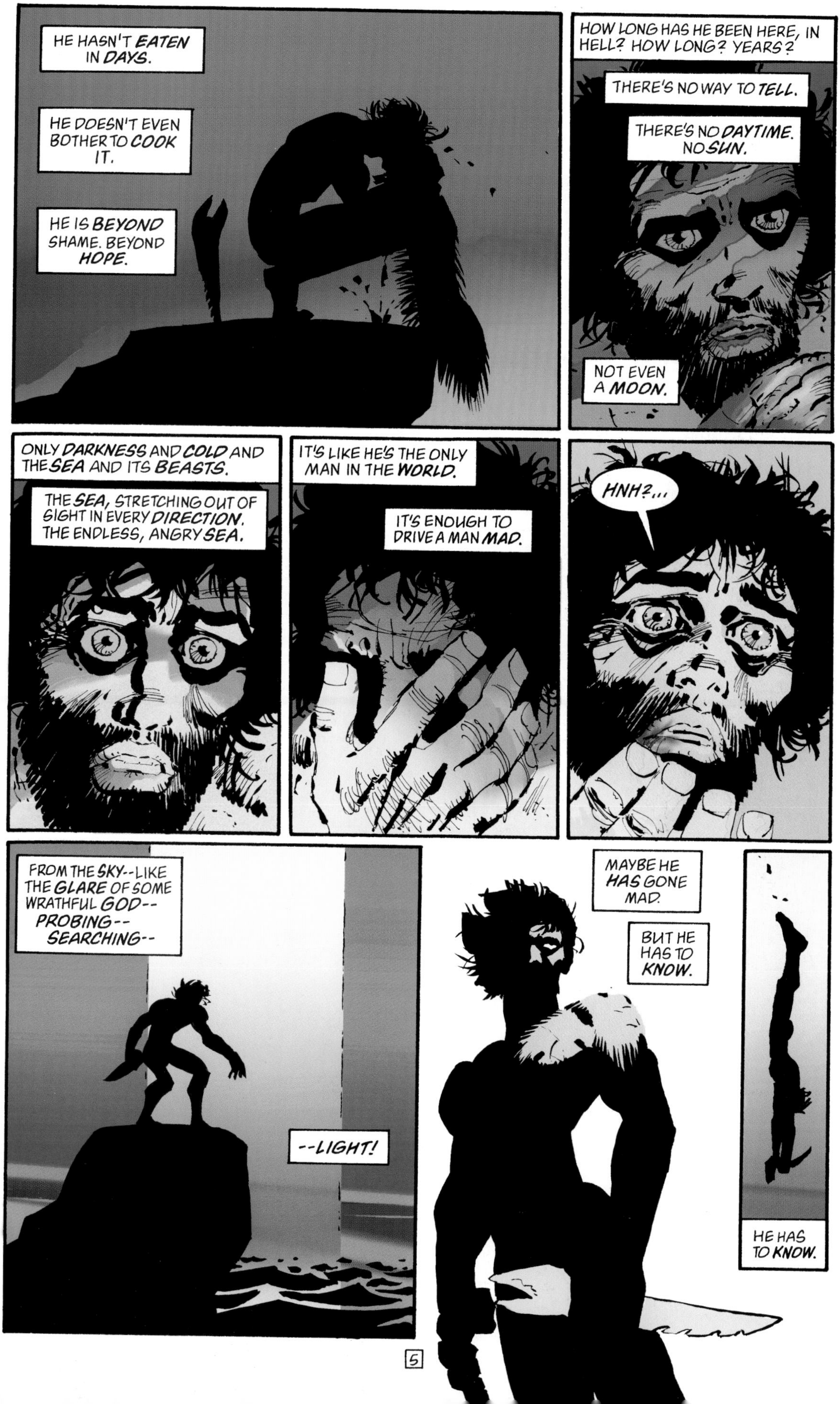
HE HASN'T EATEN IN DAYS.
HE DOESN'T EVEN BOTHER TO COOK IT.
HE IS BEYOND SHAME. BEYOND HOPE.
HOW LONG HAS HE BEEN HERE, IN HELL? HOW LONG? YEARS?
THERE'S NO WAY TO TELL.
THERE'S NO DAYTIME. NO SUN.
NOT EVEN A MOON.
ONLY DARKNESS AND COLD AND THE SEA AND ITS BEASTS.
THE SEA, STRETCHING OUT OF SIGHT IN EVERY DIRECTION. THE ENDLESS, ANGRY SEA.
IT'S LIKE HE'S THE ONLY MAN IN THE WORLD.
IT'S ENOUGH TO DRIVE A MAN MAD.
HNH?...
FROM THE SKY--LIKE THE GLARE OF SOME WRATHFUL GOD-- PROBING-- SEARCHING--
--LIGHT!
MAYBE HE HAS GONE MAD.
BUT HE HAS TO KNOW.
HE HAS TO KNOW.

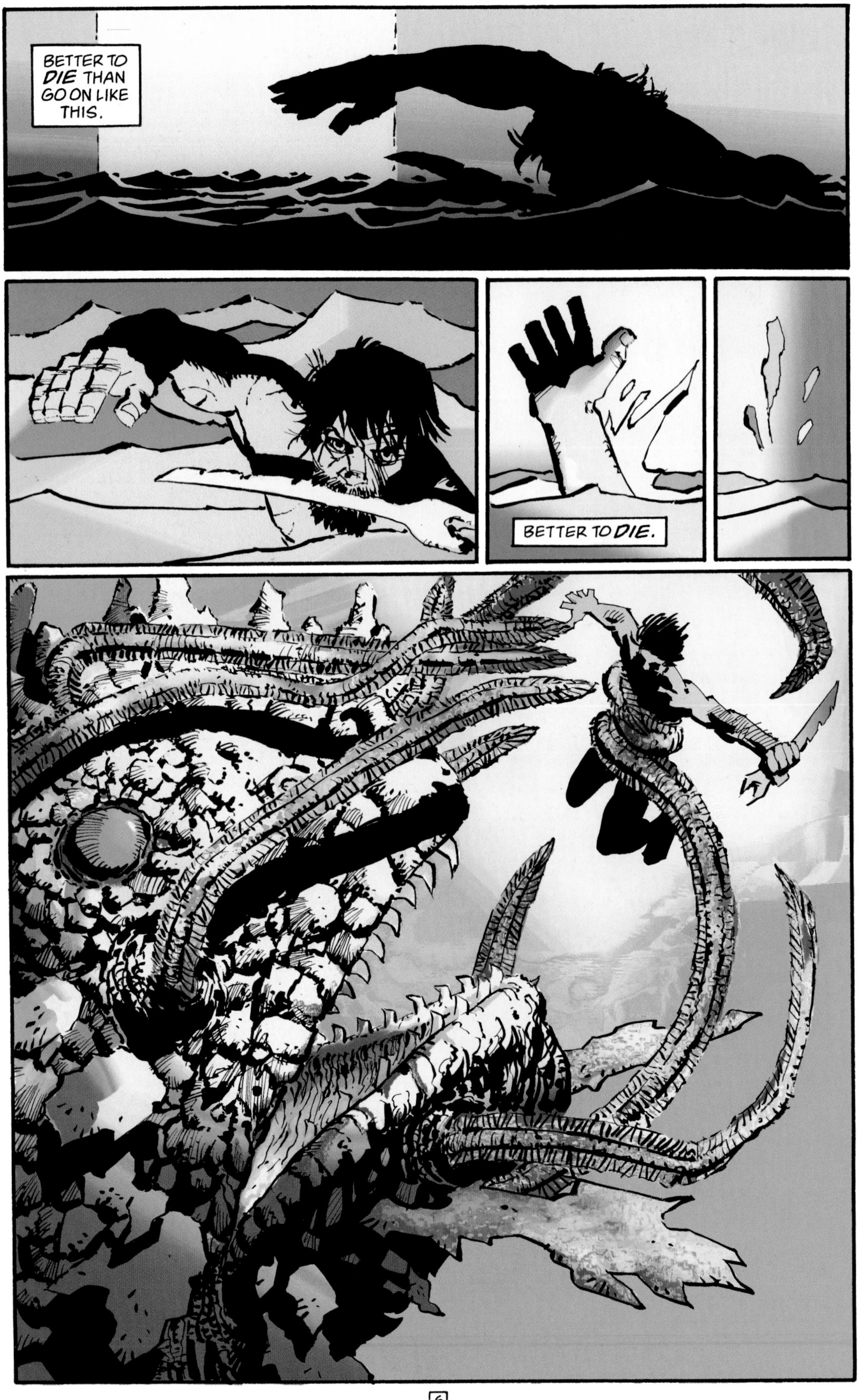
BETTER TO DIE THAN GO ON LIKE THIS.
BETTER TO DIE.

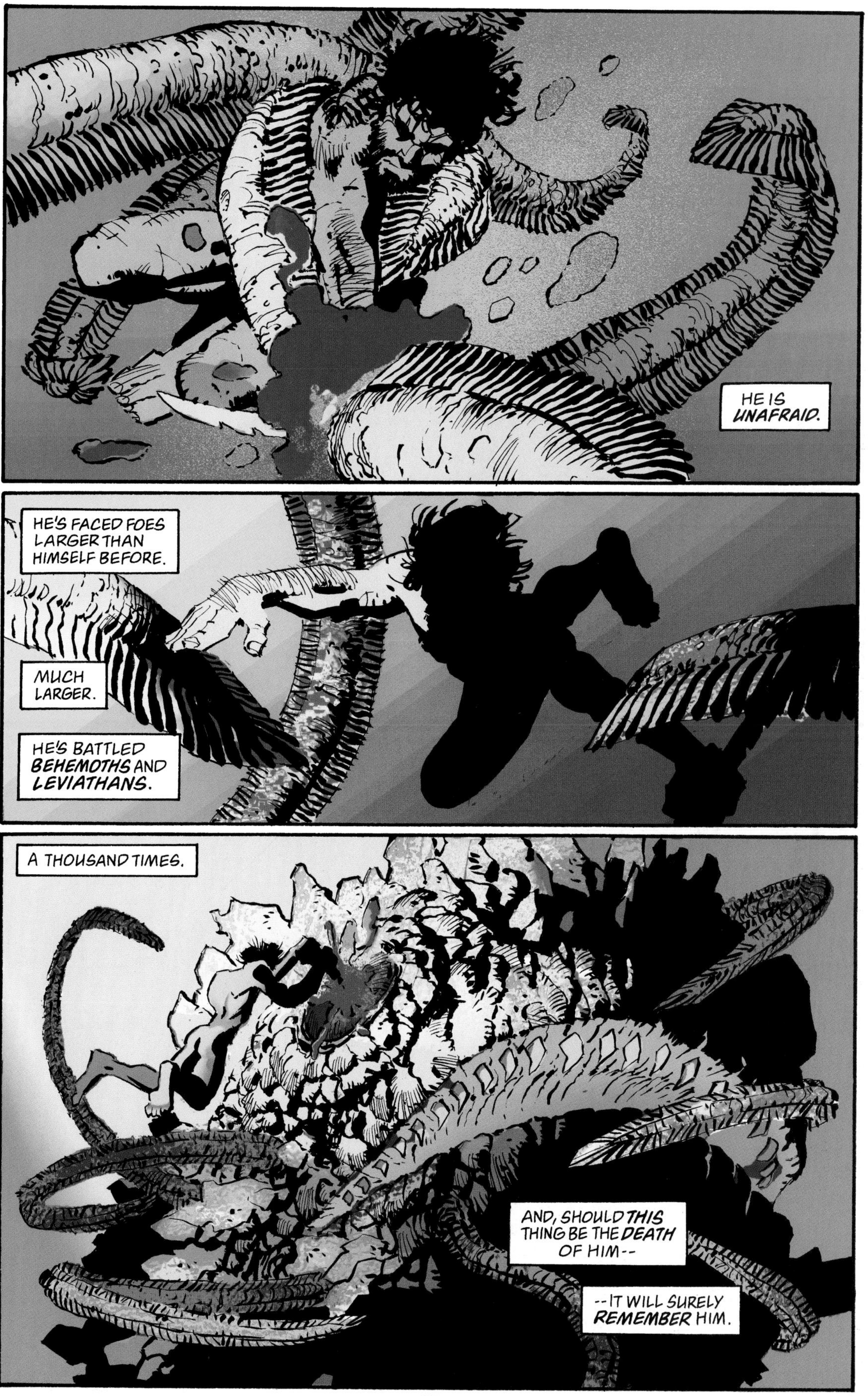
HE IS *UNAFRAID.*
HE'S FACED FOES LARGER THAN HIMSELF BEFORE.
MUCH LARGER.
HE'S BATTLED *BEHEMOTHS* AND *LEVIATHANS.*
A THOUSAND TIMES.
AND, SHOULD *THIS* THING BE THE *DEATH* OF HIM--
--IT WILL SURELY *REMEMBER* HIM.

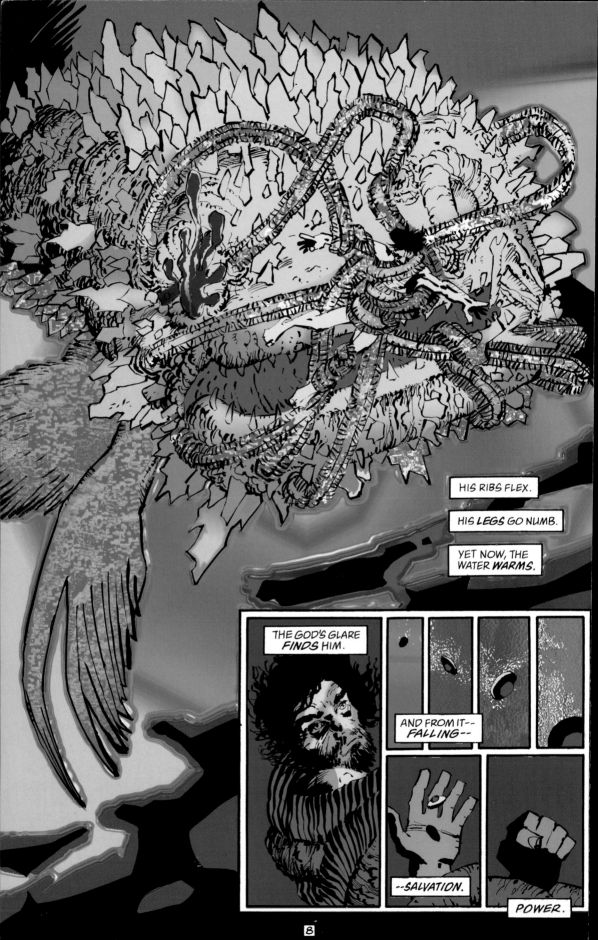

HIS RIBS FLEX.

HIS *LEGS* GO NUMB.

YET NOW, THE WATER *WARMS.*

THE GOD'S GLARE *FINDS* HIM.

AND FROM IT-- *FALLING*--

--SALVATION.

POWER.

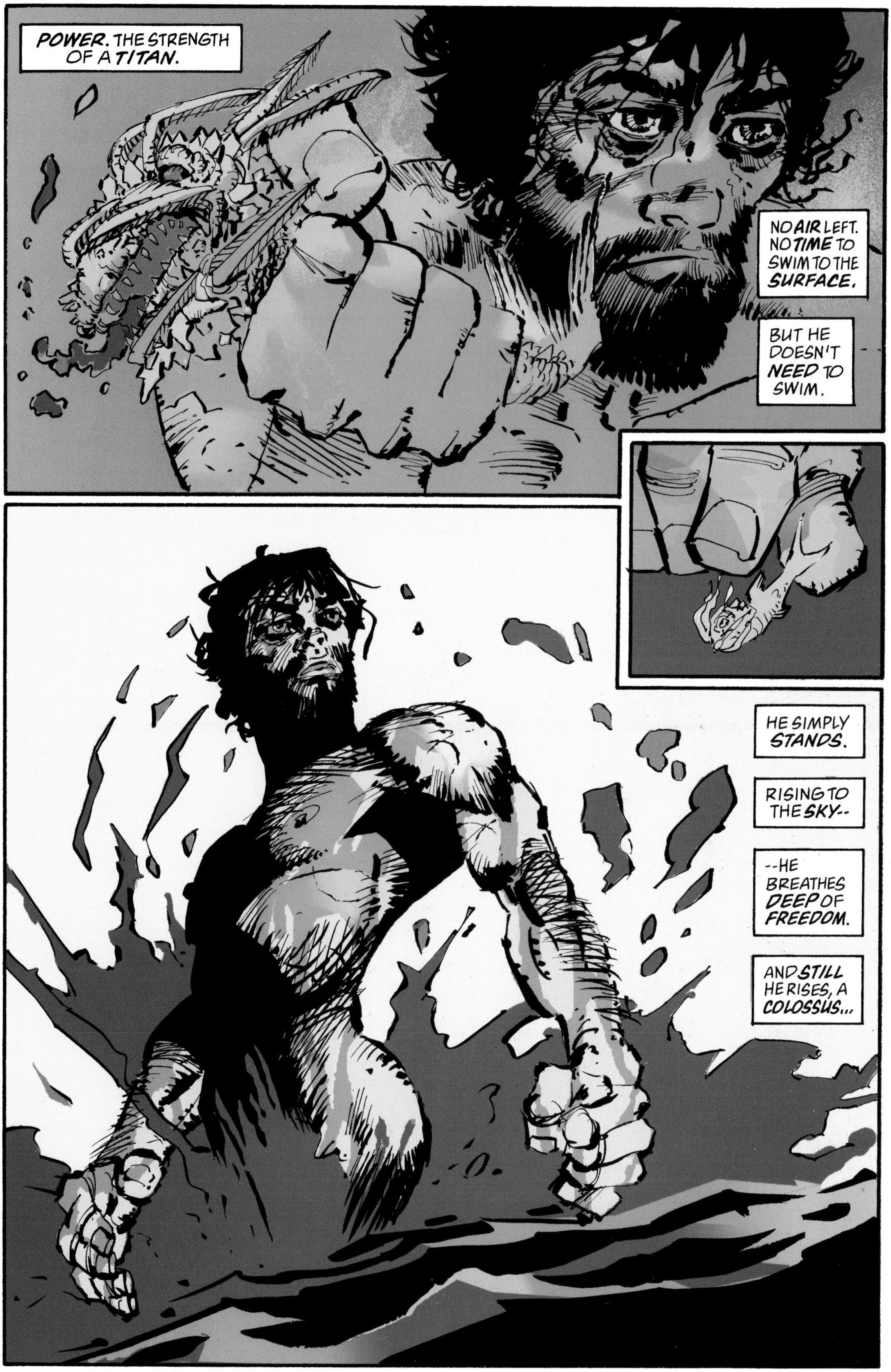
POWER. THE STRENGTH OF A TITAN.
NO AIR LEFT. NO TIME TO SWIM TO THE SURFACE.
BUT HE DOESN'T NEED TO SWIM.
HE SIMPLY STANDS.
RISING TO THE SKY--
--HE BREATHES DEEP OF FREEDOM.
AND STILL HE RISES, A COLOSSUS...

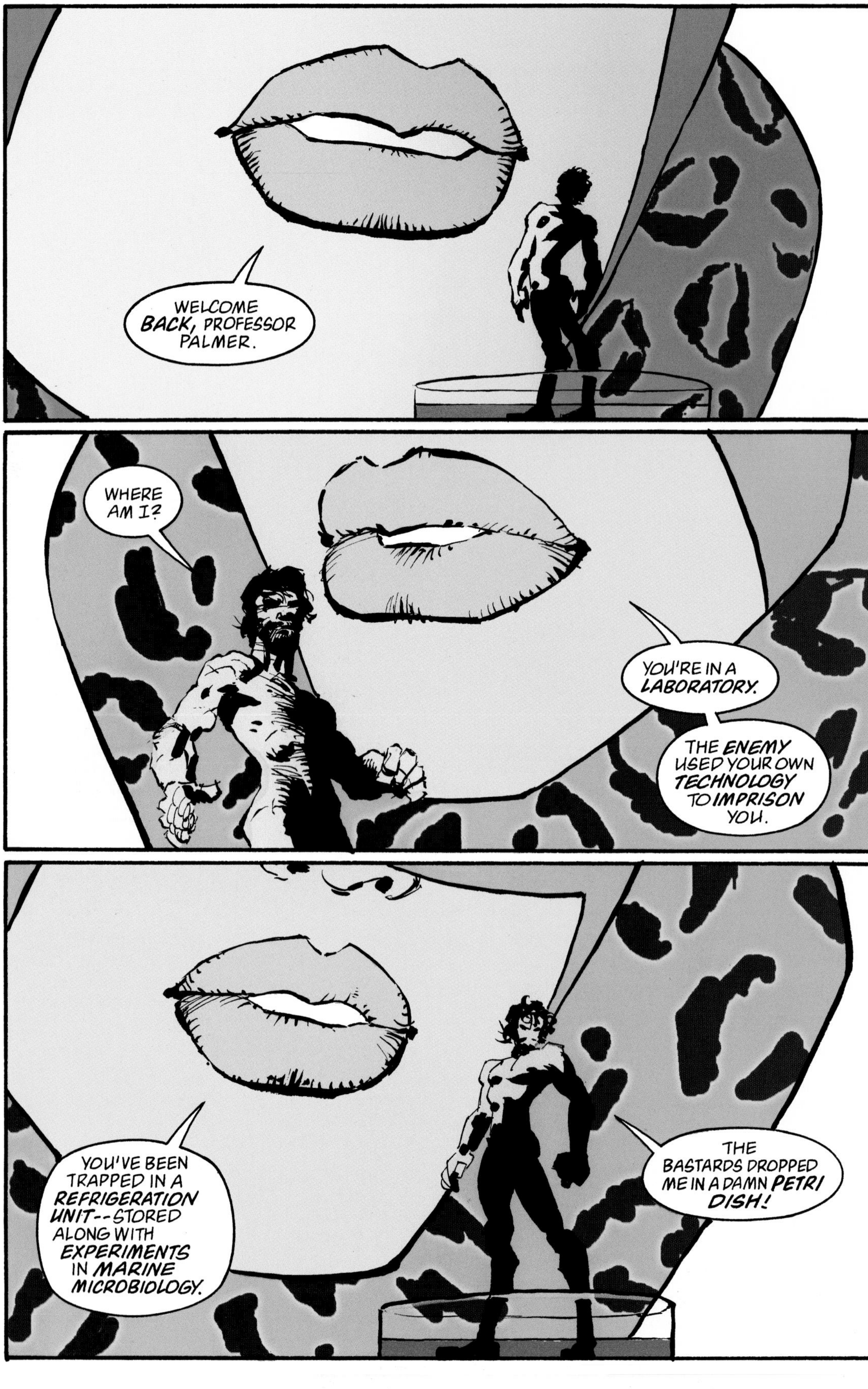
WELCOME BACK, PROFESSOR PALMER.
WHERE AM I?
YOU'RE IN A LABORATORY.
THE ENEMY USED YOUR OWN TECHNOLOGY TO IMPRISON YOU.
YOU'VE BEEN TRAPPED IN A REFRIGERATION UNIT--STORED ALONG WITH EXPERIMENTS IN MARINE MICROBIOLOGY.
THE BASTARDS DROPPED ME IN A DAMN PETRI DISH!

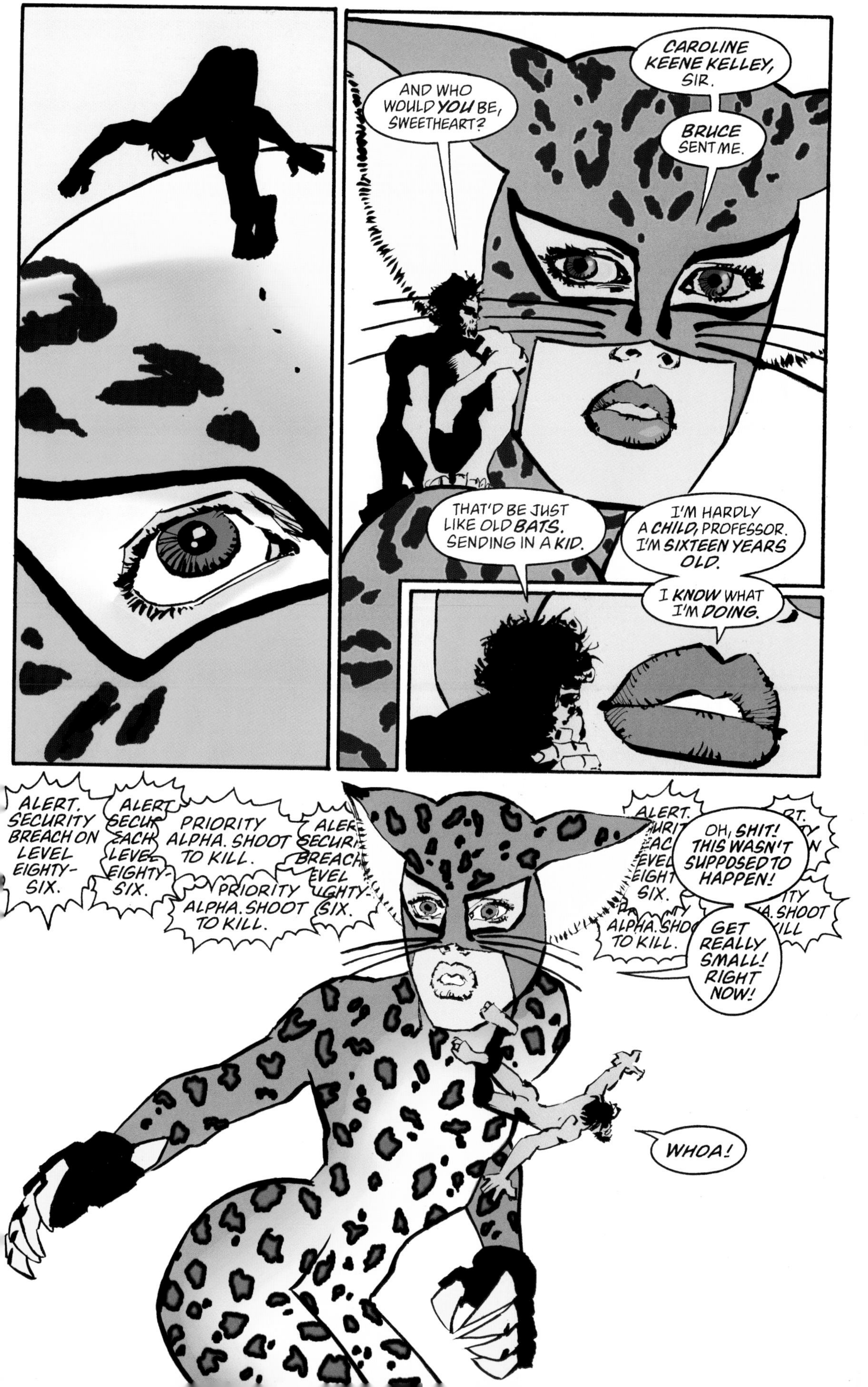
AND WHO WOULD YOU BE, SWEETHEART?
CAROLINE KEENE KELLEY, SIR.
BRUCE SENT ME.
THAT'D BE JUST LIKE OLD BATS. SENDING IN A KID.
I'M HARDLY A CHILD, PROFESSOR. I'M SIXTEEN YEARS OLD.
I KNOW WHAT I'M DOING.
ALERT. SECURITY BREACH ON LEVEL EIGHTY-SIX.
PRIORITY ALPHA. SHOOT TO KILL.
PRIORITY ALPHA. SHOOT TO KILL.
OH, SHIT! THIS WASN'T SUPPOSED TO HAPPEN!
GET REALLY SMALL! RIGHT NOW!
WHOA!

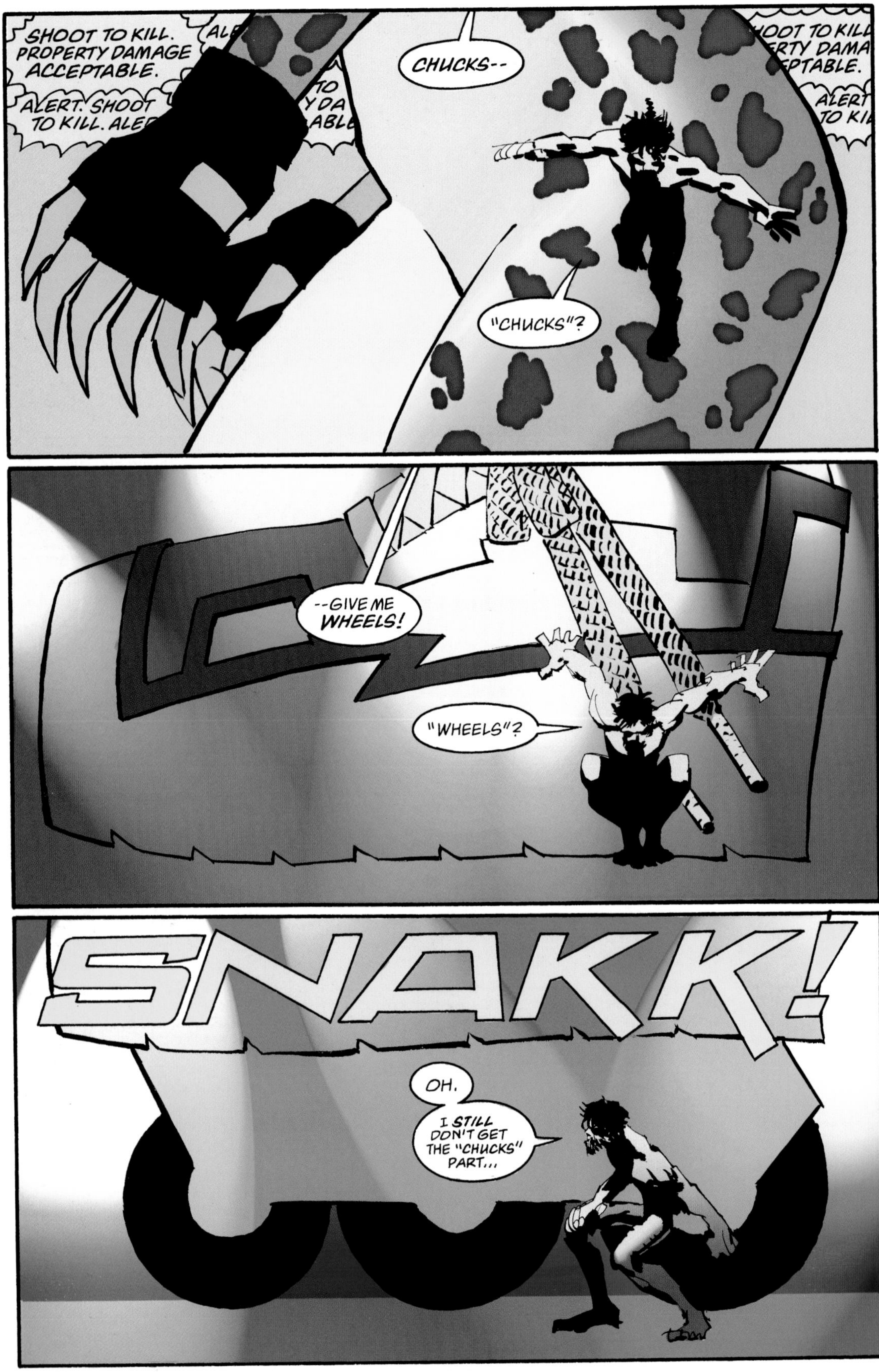
SHOOT TO KILL. PROPERTY DAMAGE ACCEPTABLE.
ALERT. SHOOT TO KILL. ALE
CHUCKS--
"CHUCKS"?
--GIVE ME WHEELS!
"WHEELS"?
SNAKK!
OH.
I STILL DON'T GET THE "CHUCKS" PART...

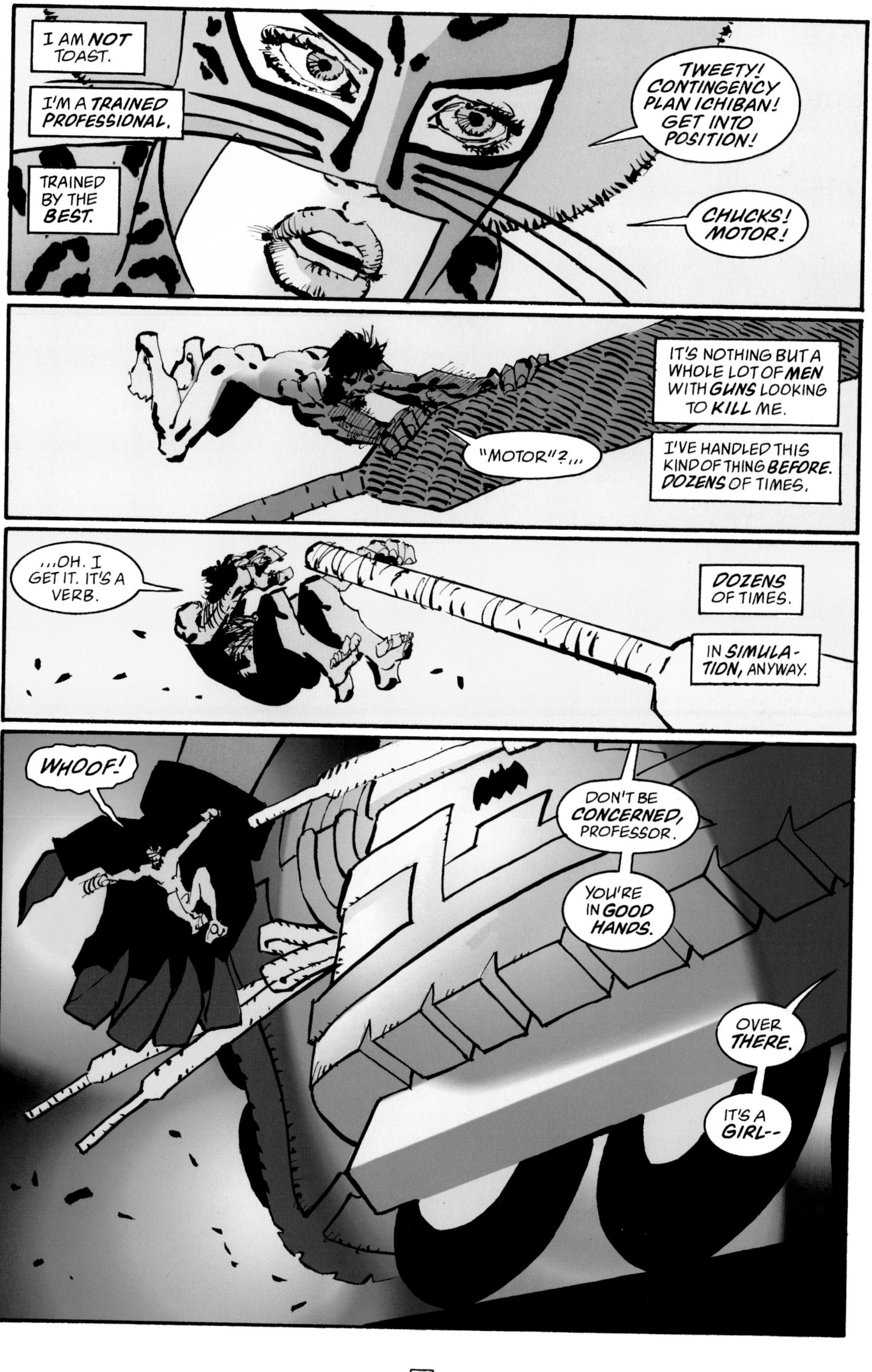
I AM NOT TOAST.
I'M A TRAINED PROFESSIONAL.
TRAINED BY THE BEST.
TWEETY! CONTINGENCY PLAN ICHIBAN! GET INTO POSITION!
CHUCKS! MOTOR!
IT'S NOTHING BUT A WHOLE LOT OF MEN WITH GUNS LOOKING TO KILL ME.
I'VE HANDLED THIS KIND OF THING BEFORE. DOZENS OF TIMES.
"MOTOR"?...
...OH. I GET IT. IT'S A VERB.
DOZENS OF TIMES.
IN SIMULATION, ANYWAY.
WHOOF!
DON'T BE CONCERNED, PROFESSOR.
YOU'RE IN GOOD HANDS.
OVER THERE.
IT'S A GIRL--

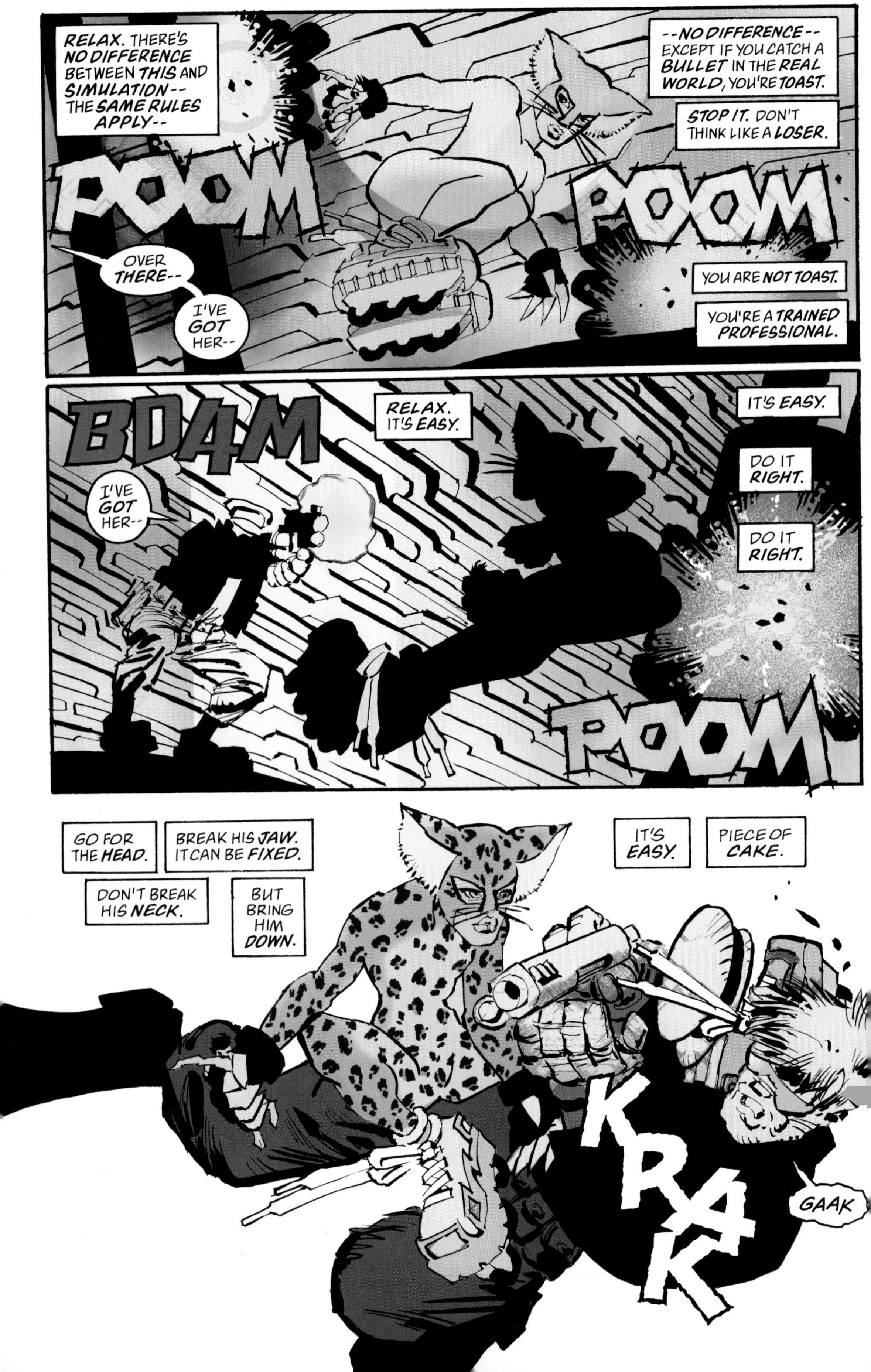

RELAX. THERE'S NO DIFFERENCE BETWEEN THIS AND SIMULATION-- THE SAME RULES APPLY--
--NO DIFFERENCE-- EXCEPT IF YOU CATCH A BULLET IN THE REAL WORLD, YOU'RE TOAST.
STOP IT. DON'T THINK LIKE A LOSER.
POOM
POOM
OVER THERE--
I'VE GOT HER--
YOU ARE NOT TOAST.
YOU'RE A TRAINED PROFESSIONAL.
BDAM
RELAX. IT'S EASY.
IT'S EASY.
I'VE GOT HER--
DO IT RIGHT.
DO IT RIGHT.
POOM
GO FOR THE HEAD.
BREAK HIS JAW. IT CAN BE FIXED.
DON'T BREAK HIS NECK.
BUT BRING HIM DOWN.
IT'S EASY.
PIECE OF CAKE.
KRAK
GAAK

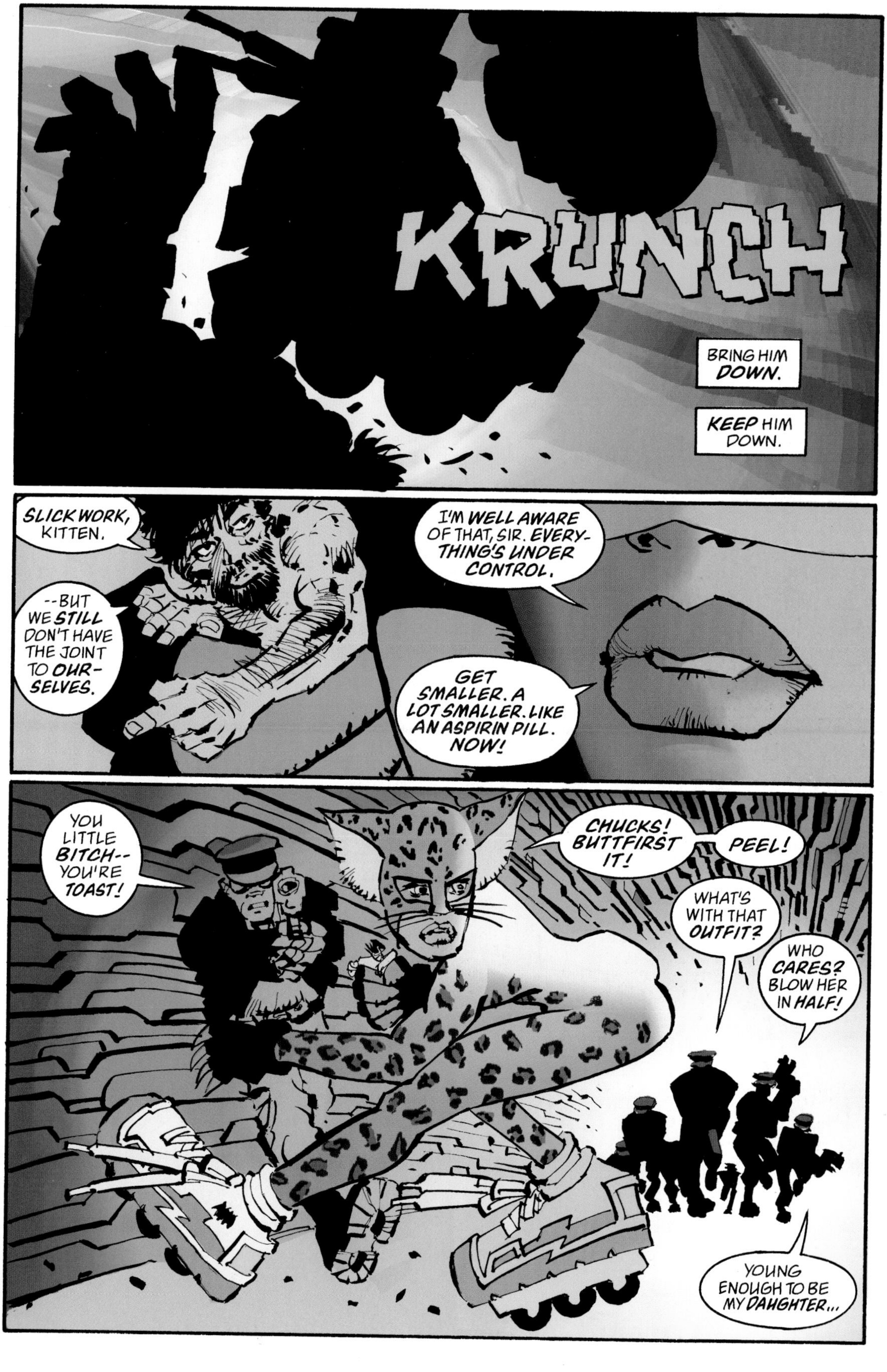
KRUNCH
BRING HIM DOWN.
KEEP HIM DOWN.
SLICK WORK, KITTEN.
--BUT WE STILL DON'T HAVE THE JOINT TO OURSELVES.
I'M WELL AWARE OF THAT, SIR. EVERYTHING'S UNDER CONTROL.
GET SMALLER. A LOT SMALLER. LIKE AN ASPIRIN PILL. NOW!
YOU LITTLE BITCH--YOU'RE TOAST!
CHUCKS! BUTTFIRST IT!
PEEL!
WHAT'S WITH THAT OUTFIT?
WHO CARES? BLOW HER IN HALF!
YOUNG ENOUGH TO BE MY DAUGHTER...

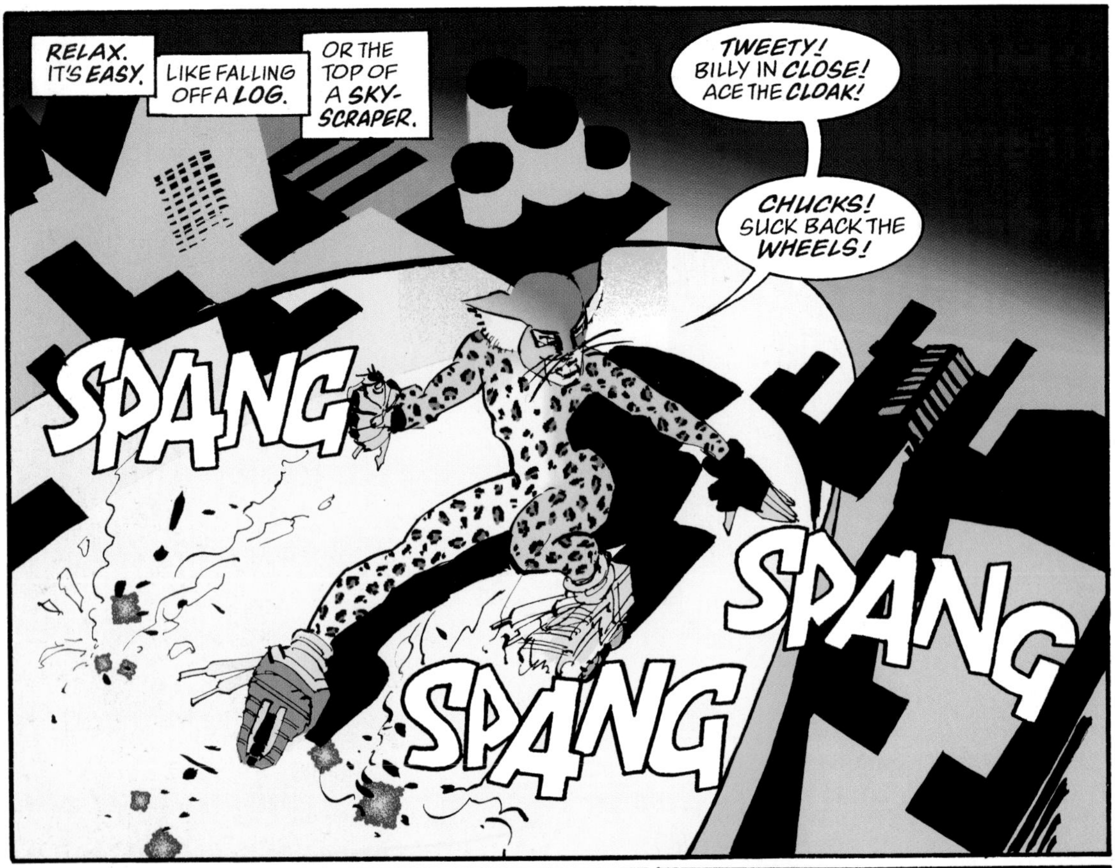
RELAX. IT'S EASY.
LIKE FALLING OFF A LOG.
OR THE TOP OF A SKY-SCRAPER.
TWEETY! BILLY IN CLOSE! ACE THE CLOAK!
CHUCKS! SUCK BACK THE WHEELS!
SPANG
SPANG
SPANG

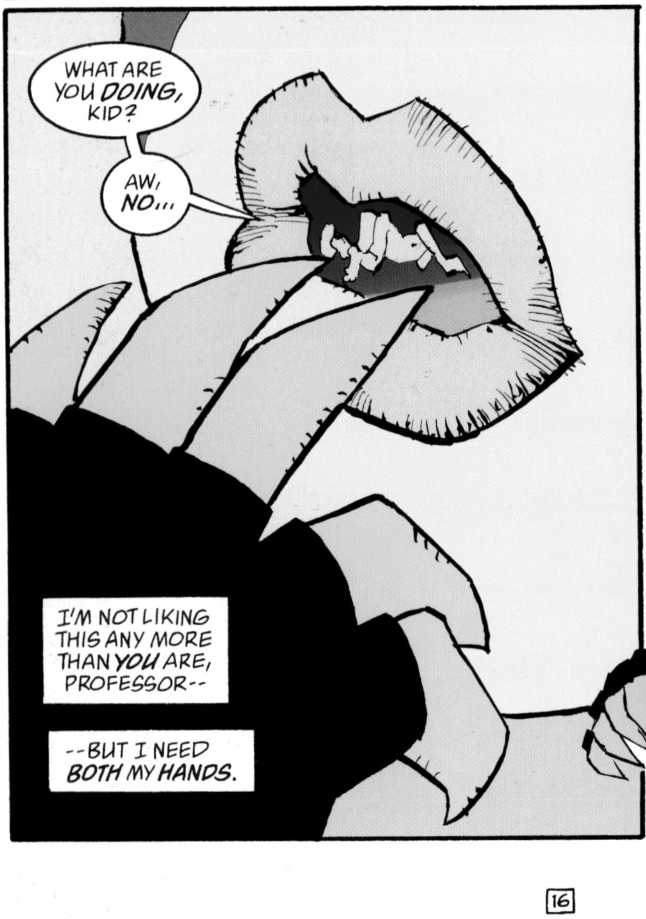
WHAT ARE YOU DOING, KID?
AW, NO...
I'M NOT LIKING THIS ANY MORE THAN YOU ARE, PROFESSOR--
--BUT I NEED BOTH MY HANDS.

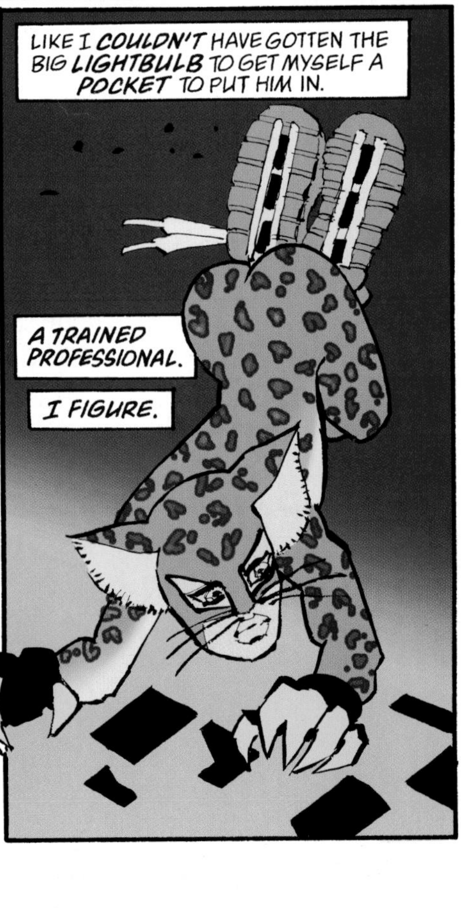
LIKE I COULDN'T HAVE GOTTEN THE BIG LIGHTBULB TO GET MYSELF A POCKET TO PUT HIM IN.
A TRAINED PROFESSIONAL.
I FIGURE.

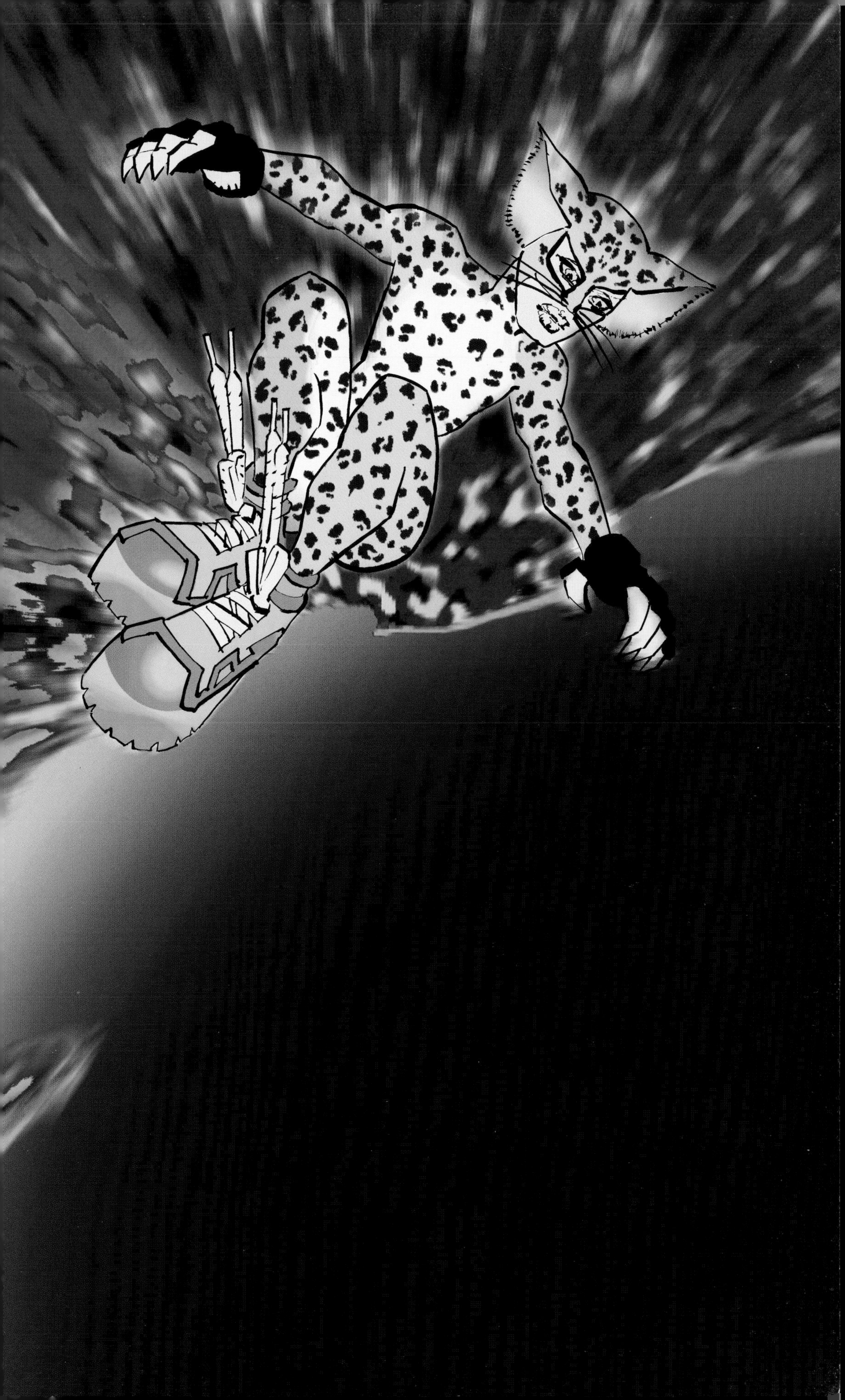

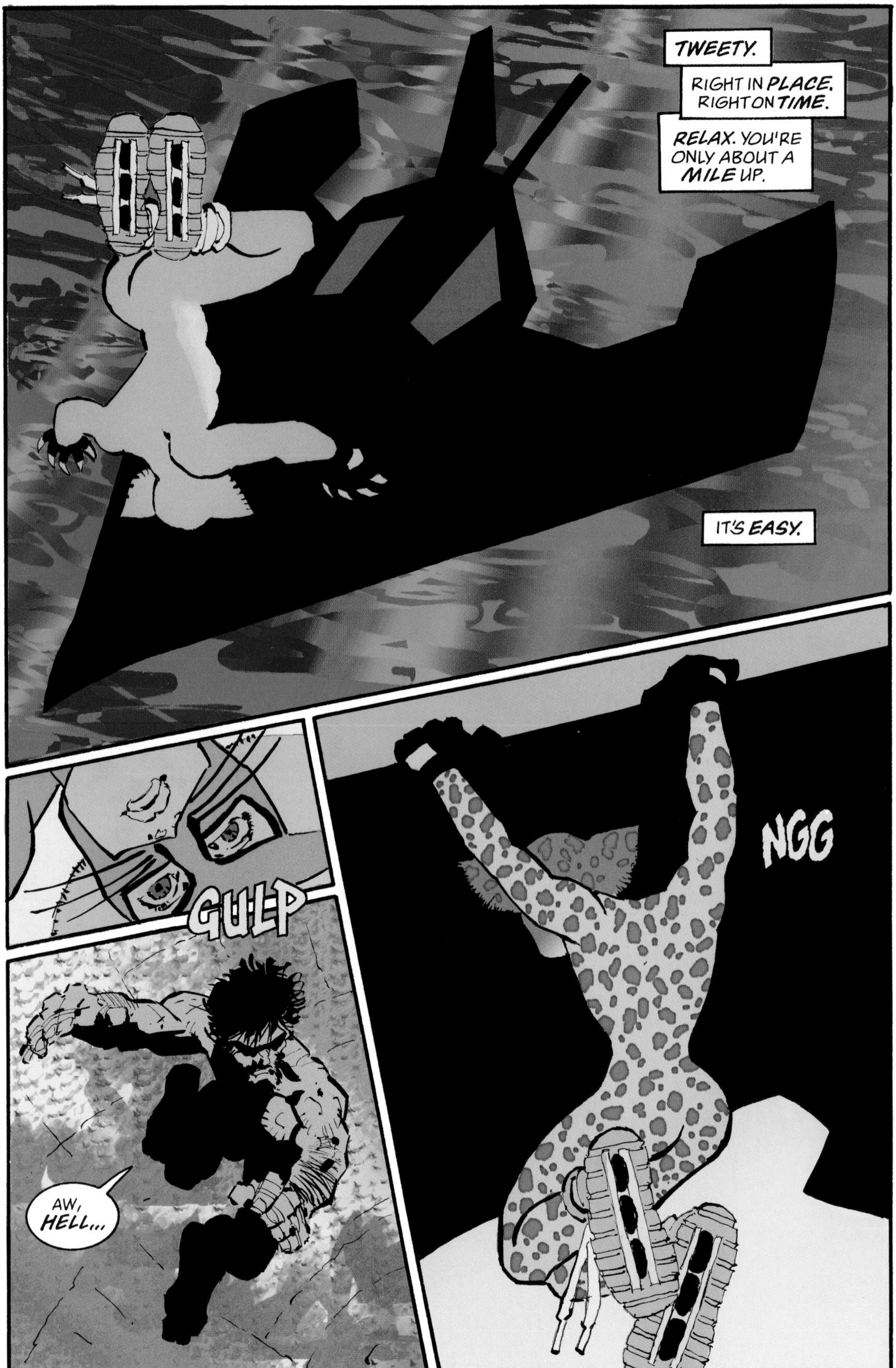
TWEETY.
RIGHT IN PLACE. RIGHT ON TIME.
RELAX. YOU'RE ONLY ABOUT A MILE UP.
IT'S EASY.
GULP
NGG
AW, HELL...

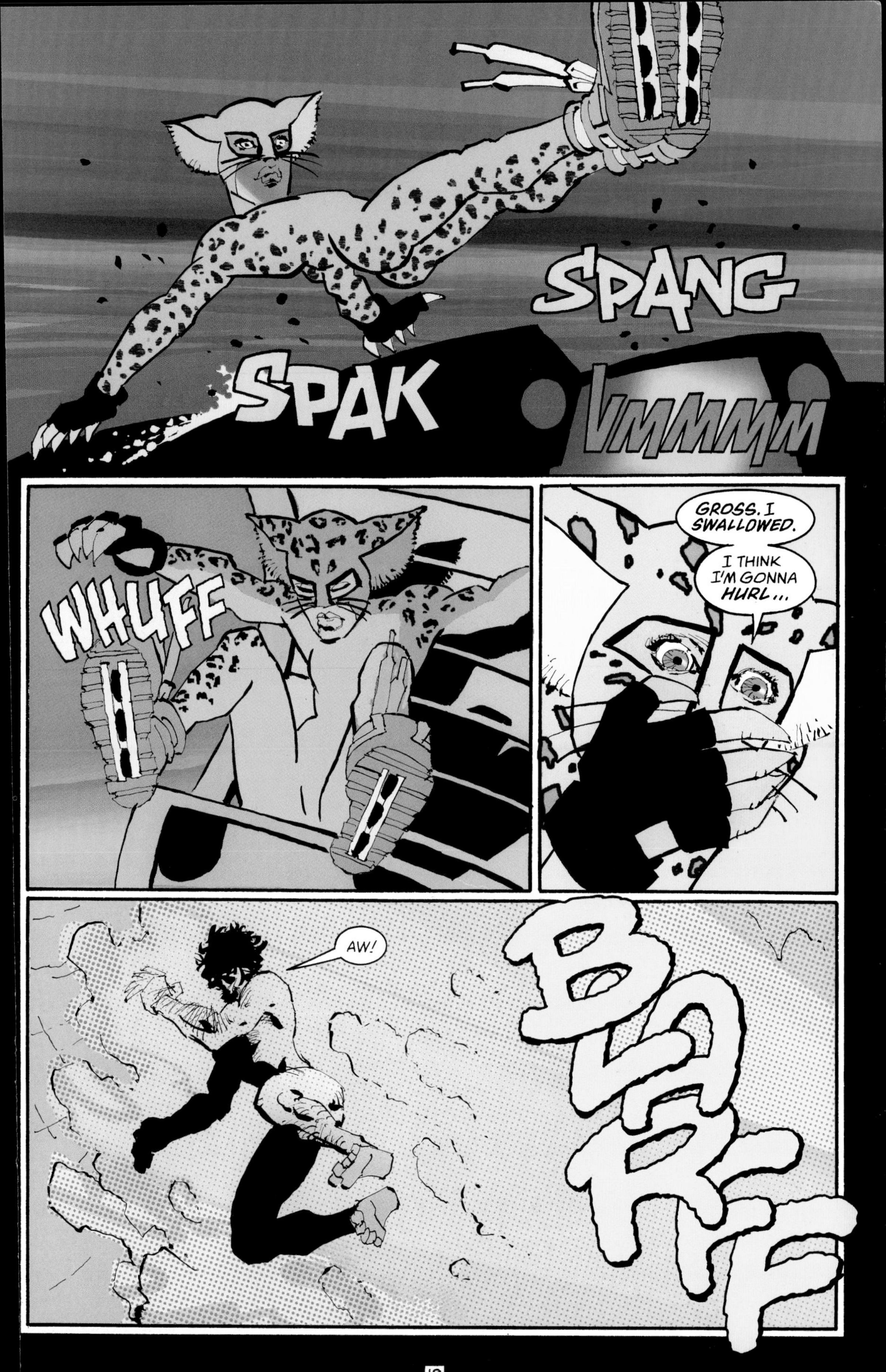
SPANG
SPAK
VMMMMM
WHUFF
GROSS. I SWALLOWED.
I THINK I'M GONNA HURL...
AW!
BLAFF

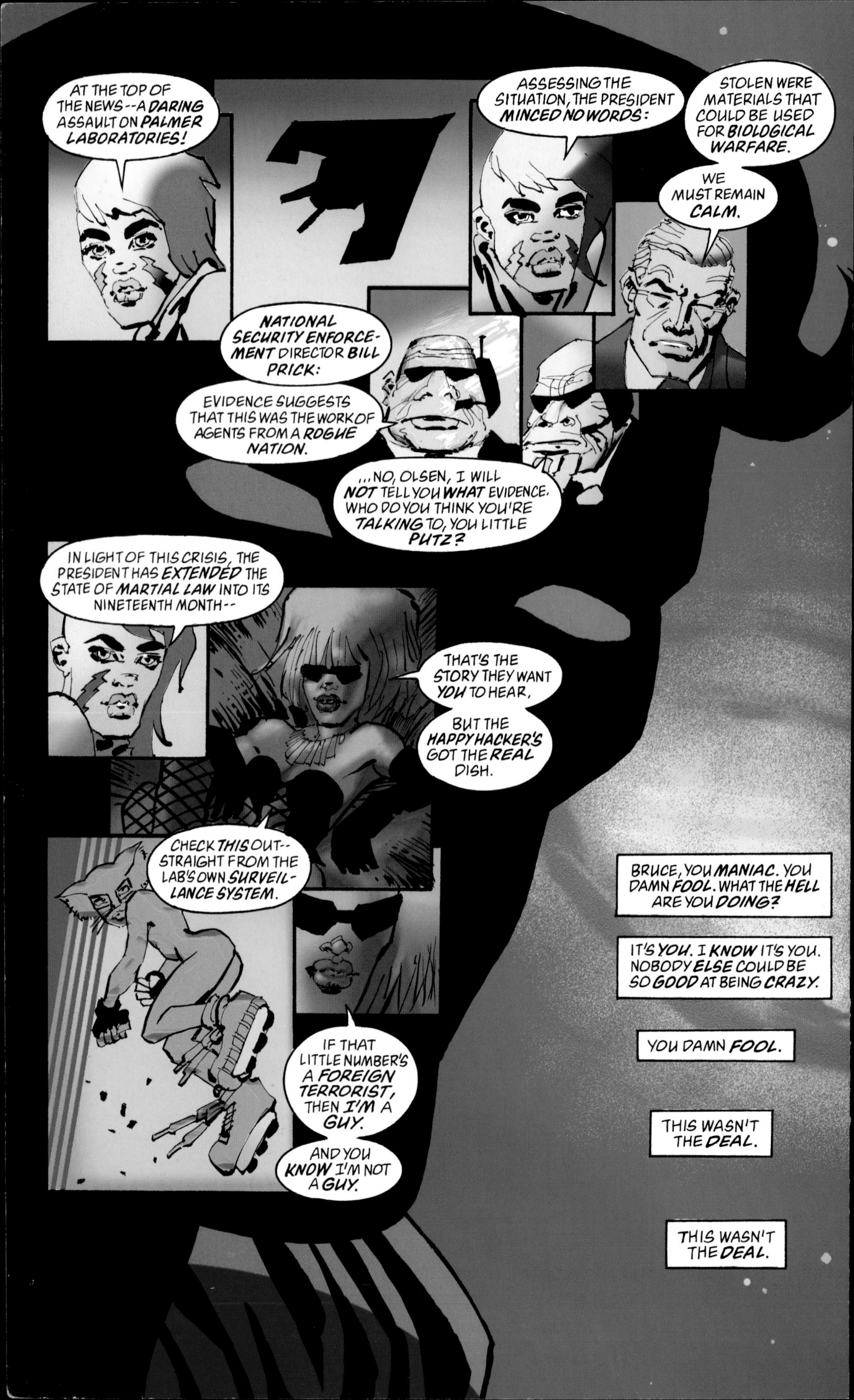

AT THE TOP OF THE NEWS--A DARING ASSAULT ON PALMER LABORATORIES!
ASSESSING THE SITUATION, THE PRESIDENT MINCED NO WORDS:
STOLEN WERE MATERIALS THAT COULD BE USED FOR BIOLOGICAL WARFARE.
WE MUST REMAIN CALM.
NATIONAL SECURITY ENFORCEMENT DIRECTOR BILL PRICK:
EVIDENCE SUGGESTS THAT THIS WAS THE WORK OF AGENTS FROM A ROGUE NATION.
...NO, OLSEN, I WILL NOT TELL YOU WHAT EVIDENCE. WHO DO YOU THINK YOU'RE TALKING TO, YOU LITTLE PUTZ?
IN LIGHT OF THIS CRISIS, THE PRESIDENT HAS EXTENDED THE STATE OF MARTIAL LAW INTO ITS NINETEENTH MONTH--
THAT'S THE STORY THEY WANT YOU TO HEAR.
BUT THE HAPPY HACKER'S GOT THE REAL DISH.
CHECK THIS OUT--STRAIGHT FROM THE LAB'S OWN SURVEILLANCE SYSTEM.
IF THAT LITTLE NUMBER'S A FOREIGN TERRORIST, THEN I'M A GUY.
AND YOU KNOW I'M NOT A GUY.
BRUCE, YOU MANIAC. YOU DAMN FOOL. WHAT THE HELL ARE YOU DOING?
IT'S YOU. I KNOW IT'S YOU. NOBODY ELSE COULD BE SO GOOD AT BEING CRAZY.
YOU DAMN FOOL.
THIS WASN'T THE DEAL.
THIS WASN'T THE DEAL.

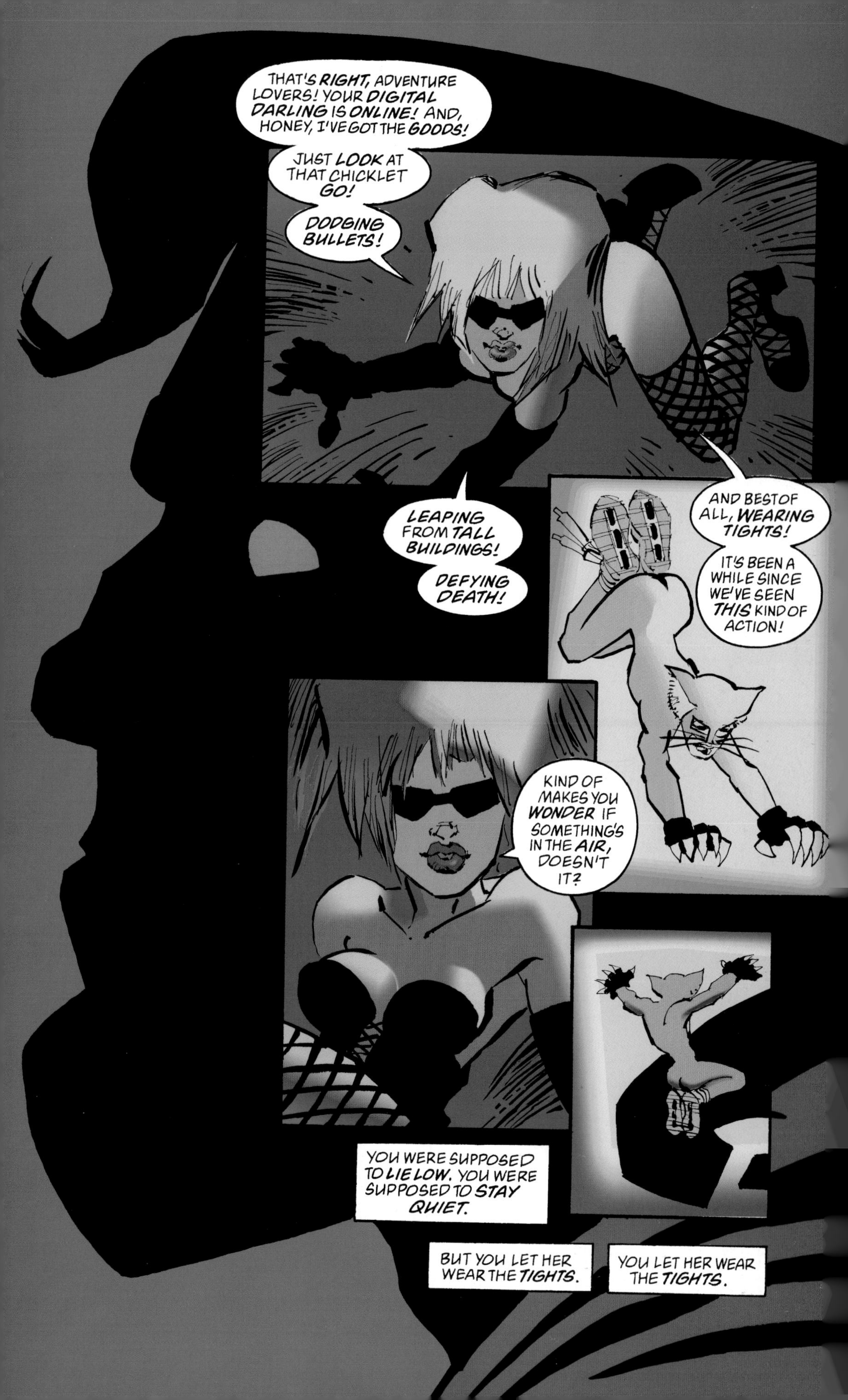
THAT'S RIGHT, ADVENTURE LOVERS! YOUR DIGITAL DARLING IS ONLINE! AND, HONEY, I'VE GOT THE GOODS!
JUST LOOK AT THAT CHICKLET GO!
DODGING BULLETS!
LEAPING FROM TALL BUILDINGS!
DEFYING DEATH!
AND BEST OF ALL, WEARING TIGHTS!
IT'S BEEN A WHILE SINCE WE'VE SEEN THIS KIND OF ACTION!
KIND OF MAKES YOU WONDER IF SOMETHING'S IN THE AIR, DOESN'T IT?
YOU WERE SUPPOSED TO LIE LOW. YOU WERE SUPPOSED TO STAY QUIET.
BUT YOU LET HER WEAR THE TIGHTS.
YOU LET HER WEAR THE TIGHTS.

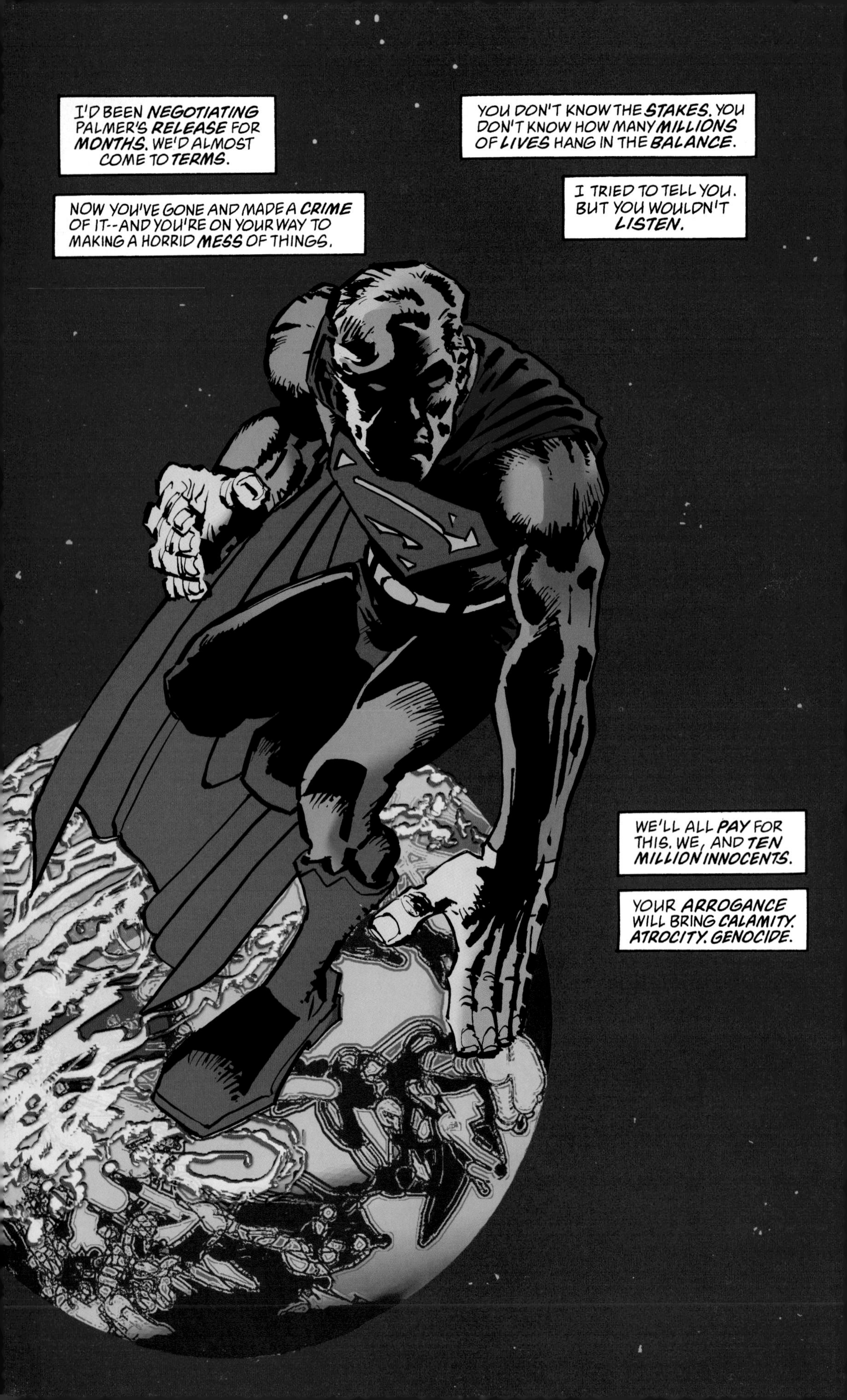
I'D BEEN NEGOTIATING PALMER'S RELEASE FOR MONTHS. WE'D ALMOST COME TO TERMS.
NOW YOU'VE GONE AND MADE A CRIME OF IT--AND YOU'RE ON YOUR WAY TO MAKING A HORRID MESS OF THINGS.
YOU DON'T KNOW THE STAKES. YOU DON'T KNOW HOW MANY MILLIONS OF LIVES HANG IN THE BALANCE.
I TRIED TO TELL YOU. BUT YOU WOULDN'T LISTEN.
WE'LL ALL PAY FOR THIS. WE, AND TEN MILLION INNOCENTS.
YOUR ARROGANCE WILL BRING CALAMITY. ATROCITY. GENOCIDE.

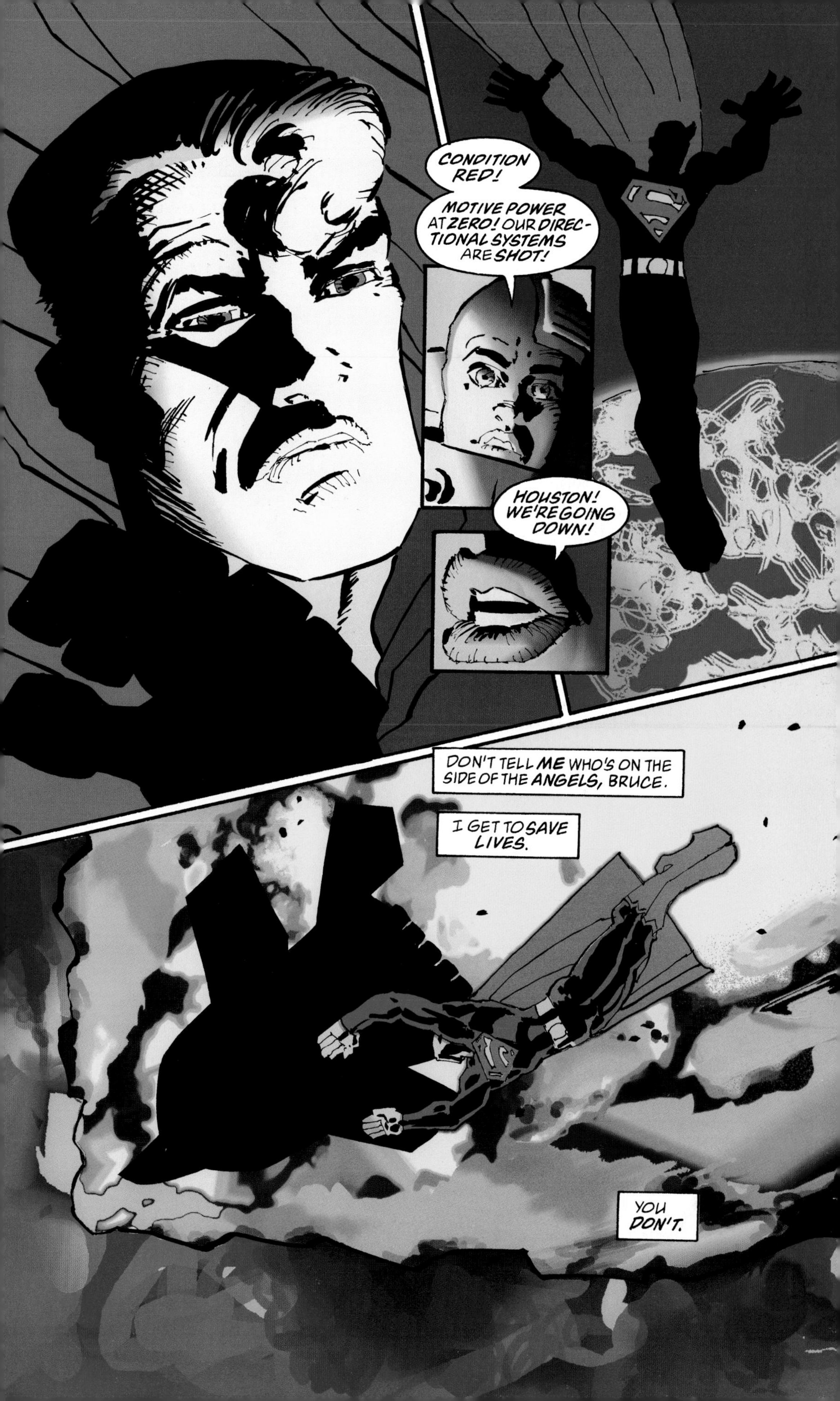
CONDITION RED!
MOTIVE POWER AT ZERO! OUR DIRECTIONAL SYSTEMS ARE SHOT!
HOUSTON! WE'RE GOING DOWN!
DON'T TELL ME WHO'S ON THE SIDE OF THE ANGELS, BRUCE.
I GET TO SAVE LIVES.
YOU DON'T.

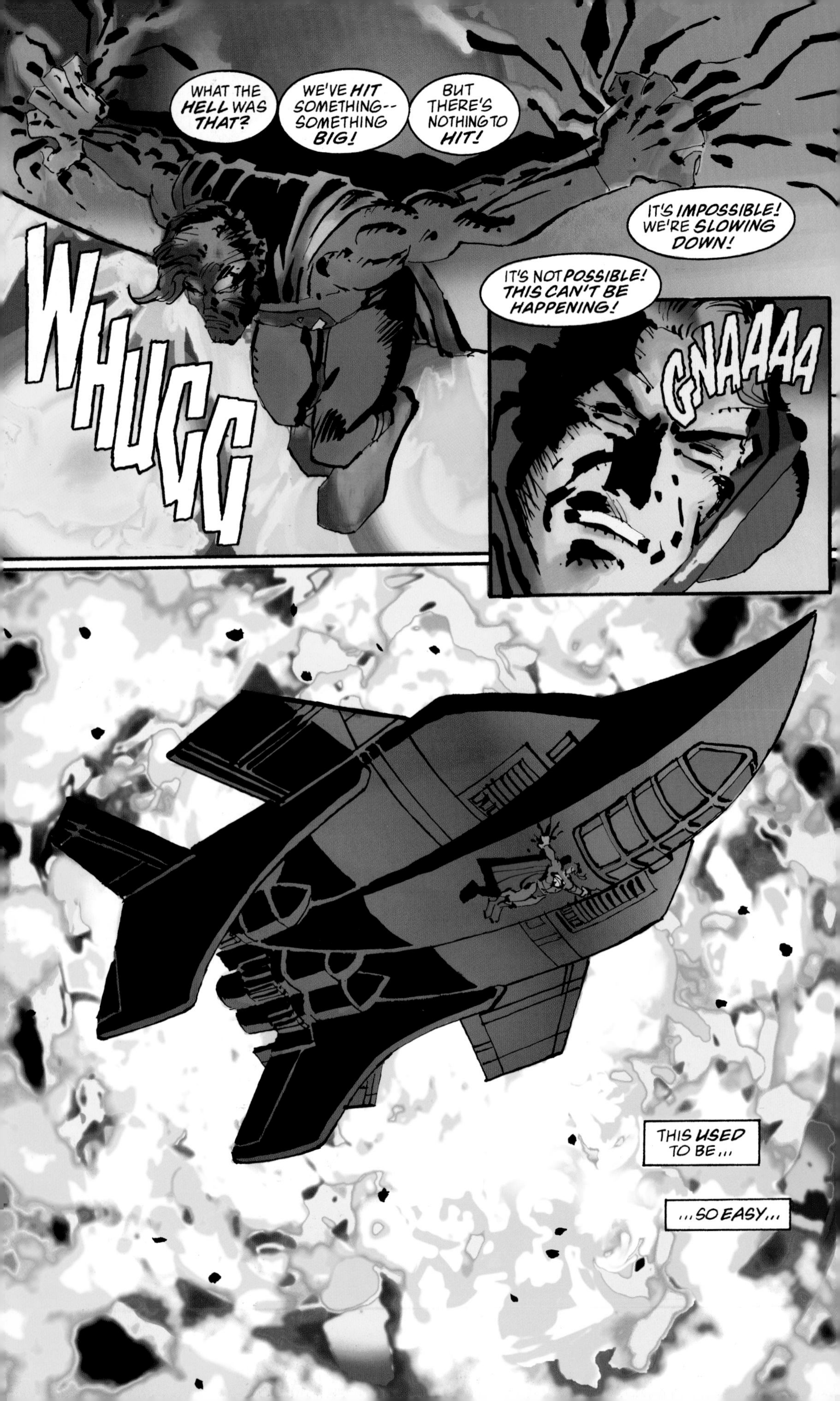
WHAT THE HELL WAS THAT?
WE'VE HIT SOMETHING-- SOMETHING BIG!
BUT THERE'S NOTHING TO HIT!
WHUGG
IT'S IMPOSSIBLE! WE'RE SLOWING DOWN!
IT'S NOT POSSIBLE! THIS CAN'T BE HAPPENING!
GNAAAA
THIS USED TO BE...
...SO EASY...

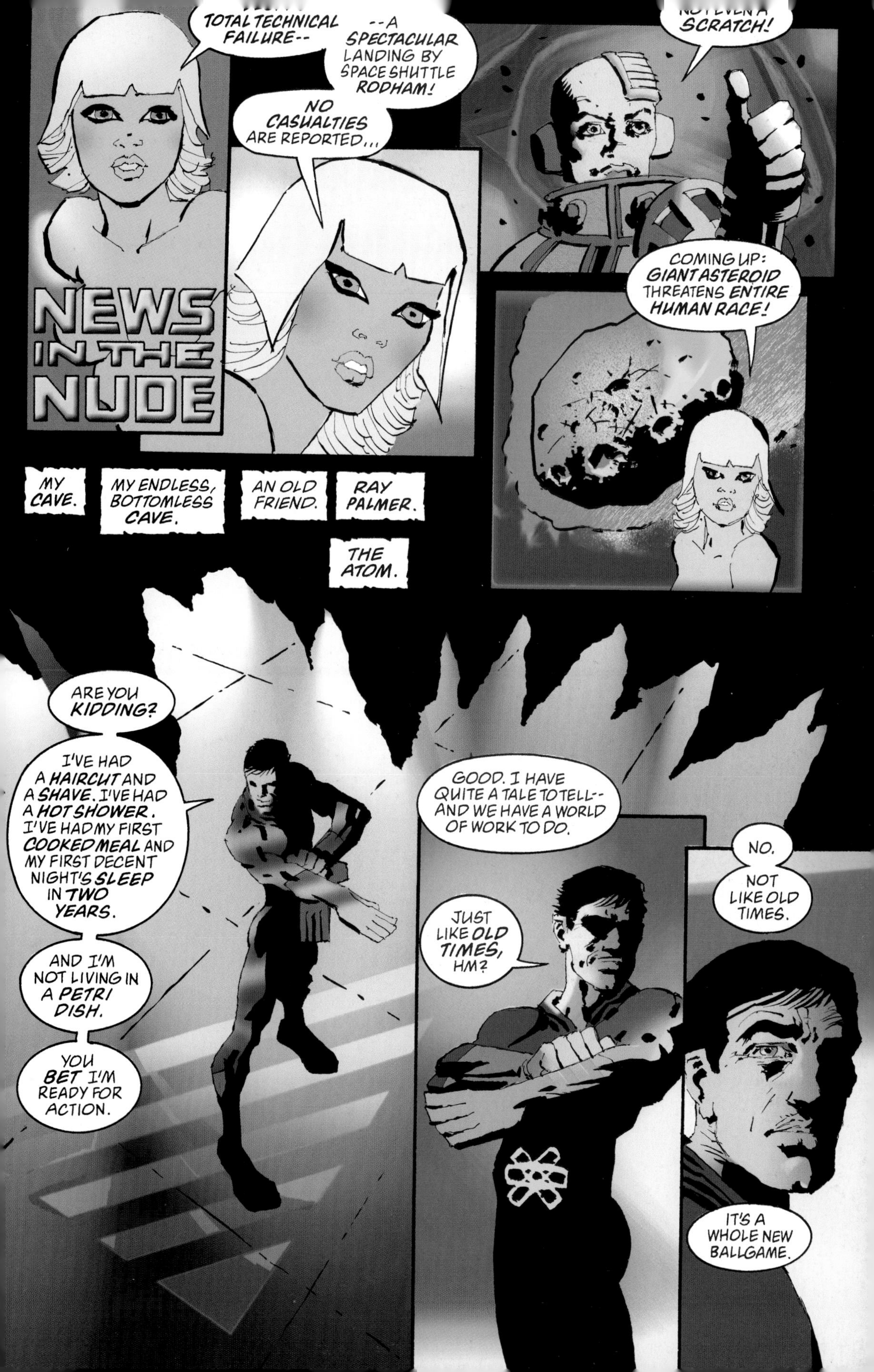

TOTAL TECHNICAL FAILURE--
--A SPECTACULAR LANDING BY SPACE SHUTTLE RODHAM!
NO CASUALTIES ARE REPORTED...
SCRATCH!
NEWS IN THE NUDE
COMING UP: GIANT ASTEROID THREATENS ENTIRE HUMAN RACE!
MY CAVE.
MY ENDLESS, BOTTOMLESS CAVE.
AN OLD FRIEND.
RAY PALMER.
THE ATOM.
ARE YOU KIDDING?
I'VE HAD A HAIRCUT AND A SHAVE. I'VE HAD A HOT SHOWER. I'VE HAD MY FIRST COOKED MEAL AND MY FIRST DECENT NIGHT'S SLEEP IN TWO YEARS.
AND I'M NOT LIVING IN A PETRI DISH.
YOU BET I'M READY FOR ACTION.
GOOD. I HAVE QUITE A TALE TO TELL-- AND WE HAVE A WORLD OF WORK TO DO.
JUST LIKE OLD TIMES, HM?
NO.
NOT LIKE OLD TIMES.
IT'S A WHOLE NEW BALLGAME.

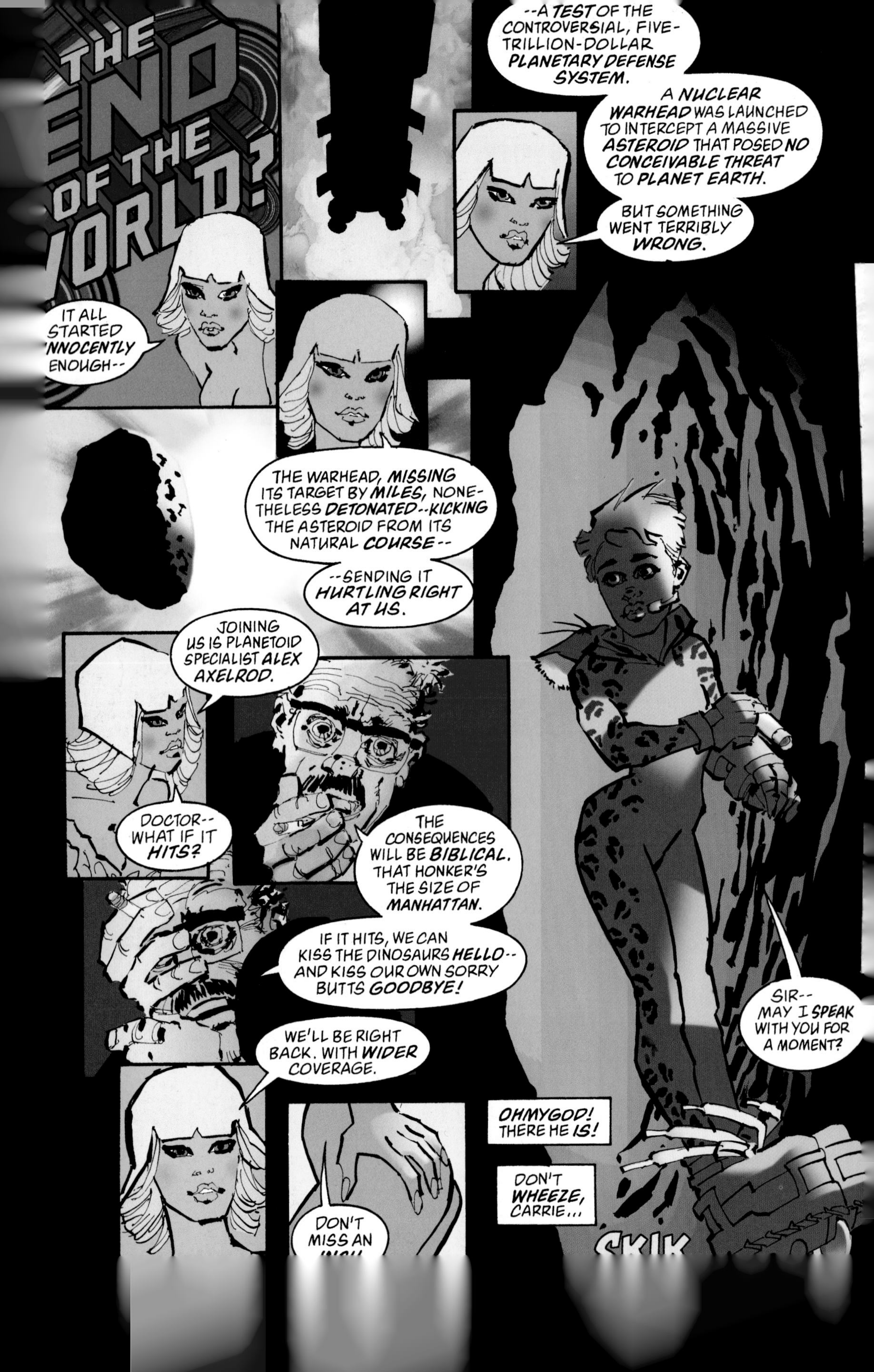
THE END OF THE WORLD?
IT ALL STARTED INNOCENTLY ENOUGH--
--A TEST OF THE CONTROVERSIAL, FIVE-TRILLION-DOLLAR PLANETARY DEFENSE SYSTEM.
A NUCLEAR WARHEAD WAS LAUNCHED TO INTERCEPT A MASSIVE ASTEROID THAT POSED NO CONCEIVABLE THREAT TO PLANET EARTH.
BUT SOMETHING WENT TERRIBLY WRONG.
THE WARHEAD, MISSING ITS TARGET BY MILES, NONETHELESS DETONATED--KICKING THE ASTEROID FROM ITS NATURAL COURSE--
--SENDING IT HURTLING RIGHT AT US.
JOINING US IS PLANETOID SPECIALIST ALEX AXELROD.
DOCTOR--WHAT IF IT HITS?
THE CONSEQUENCES WILL BE BIBLICAL. THAT HONKER'S THE SIZE OF MANHATTAN.
IF IT HITS, WE CAN KISS THE DINOSAURS HELLO--AND KISS OUR OWN SORRY BUTTS GOODBYE!
WE'LL BE RIGHT BACK. WITH WIDER COVERAGE.
DON'T MISS AN
SIR--MAY I SPEAK WITH YOU FOR A MOMENT?
OHMYGOD! THERE HE IS!
DON'T WHEEZE, CARRIE...
SKIK

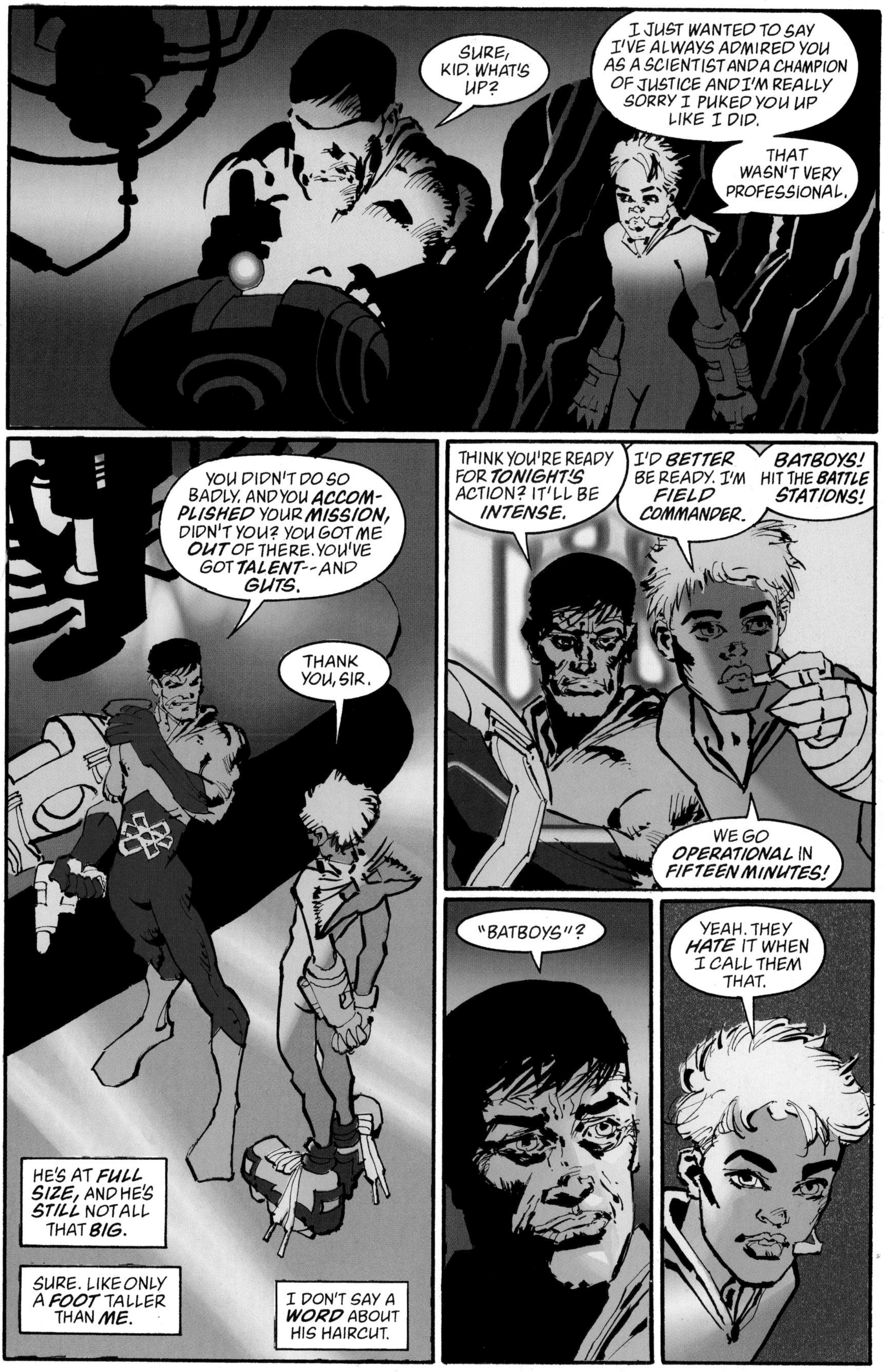

SURE, KID. WHAT'S UP?
I JUST WANTED TO SAY I'VE ALWAYS ADMIRED YOU AS A SCIENTIST AND A CHAMPION OF JUSTICE AND I'M REALLY SORRY I PUKED YOU UP LIKE I DID.
THAT WASN'T VERY PROFESSIONAL.
YOU DIDN'T DO SO BADLY. AND YOU ACCOMPLISHED YOUR MISSION, DIDN'T YOU? YOU GOT ME OUT OF THERE. YOU'VE GOT TALENT--AND GUTS.
THANK YOU, SIR.
HE'S AT FULL SIZE, AND HE'S STILL NOT ALL THAT BIG.
SURE. LIKE ONLY A FOOT TALLER THAN ME.
I DON'T SAY A WORD ABOUT HIS HAIRCUT.
THINK YOU'RE READY FOR TONIGHT'S ACTION? IT'LL BE INTENSE.
I'D BETTER BE READY. I'M FIELD COMMANDER.
BATBOYS! HIT THE BATTLE STATIONS!
WE GO OPERATIONAL IN FIFTEEN MINUTES!
"BATBOYS"?
YEAH. THEY HATE IT WHEN I CALL THEM THAT.

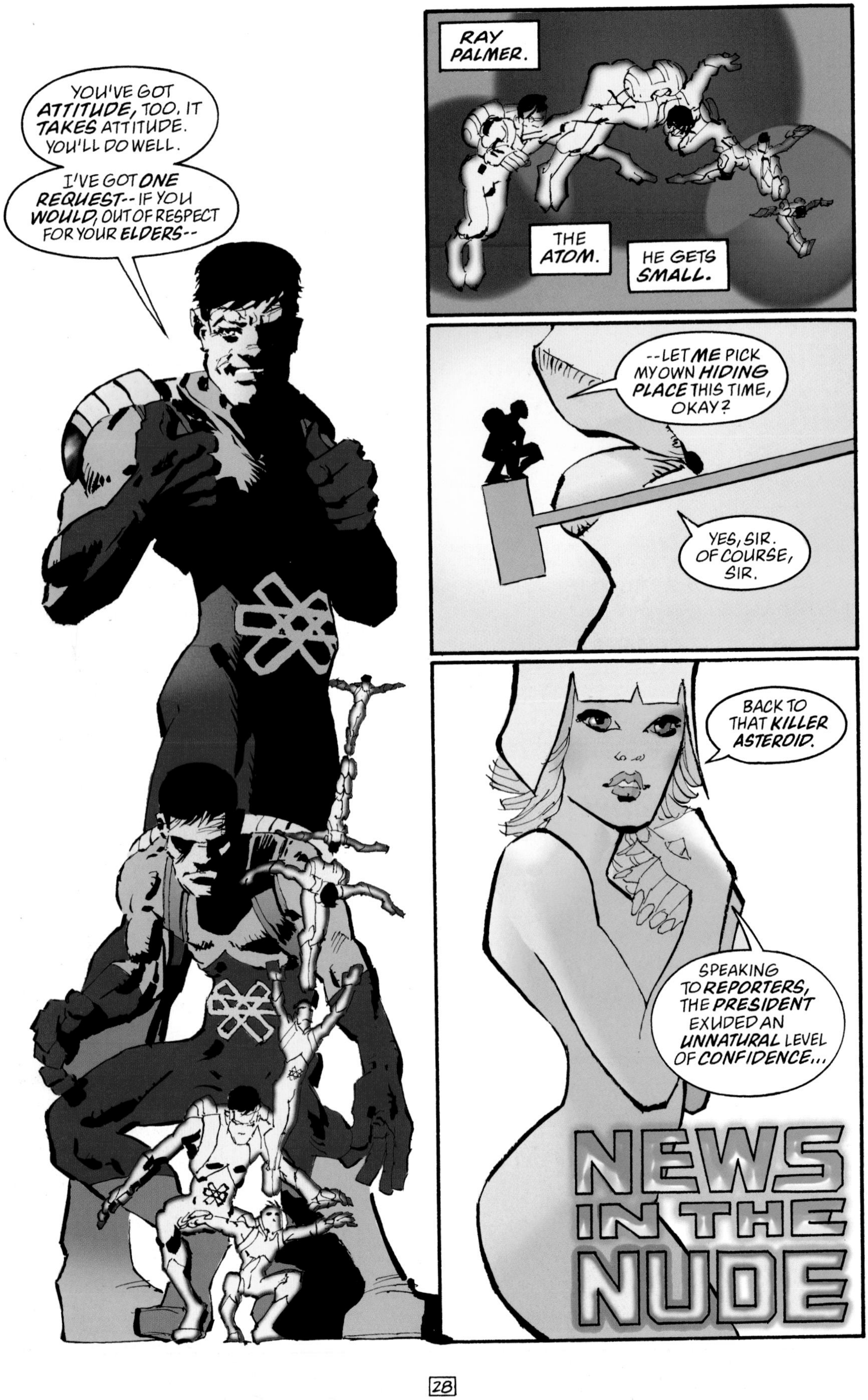
YOU'VE GOT ATTITUDE, TOO. IT TAKES ATTITUDE. YOU'LL DO WELL.
I'VE GOT ONE REQUEST-- IF YOU WOULD, OUT OF RESPECT FOR YOUR ELDERS--
RAY PALMER.
THE ATOM.
HE GETS SMALL.
--LET ME PICK MY OWN HIDING PLACE THIS TIME, OKAY?
YES, SIR. OF COURSE, SIR.
BACK TO THAT KILLER ASTEROID.
SPEAKING TO REPORTERS, THE PRESIDENT EXUDED AN UNNATURAL LEVEL OF CONFIDENCE...
NEWS IN THE NUDE

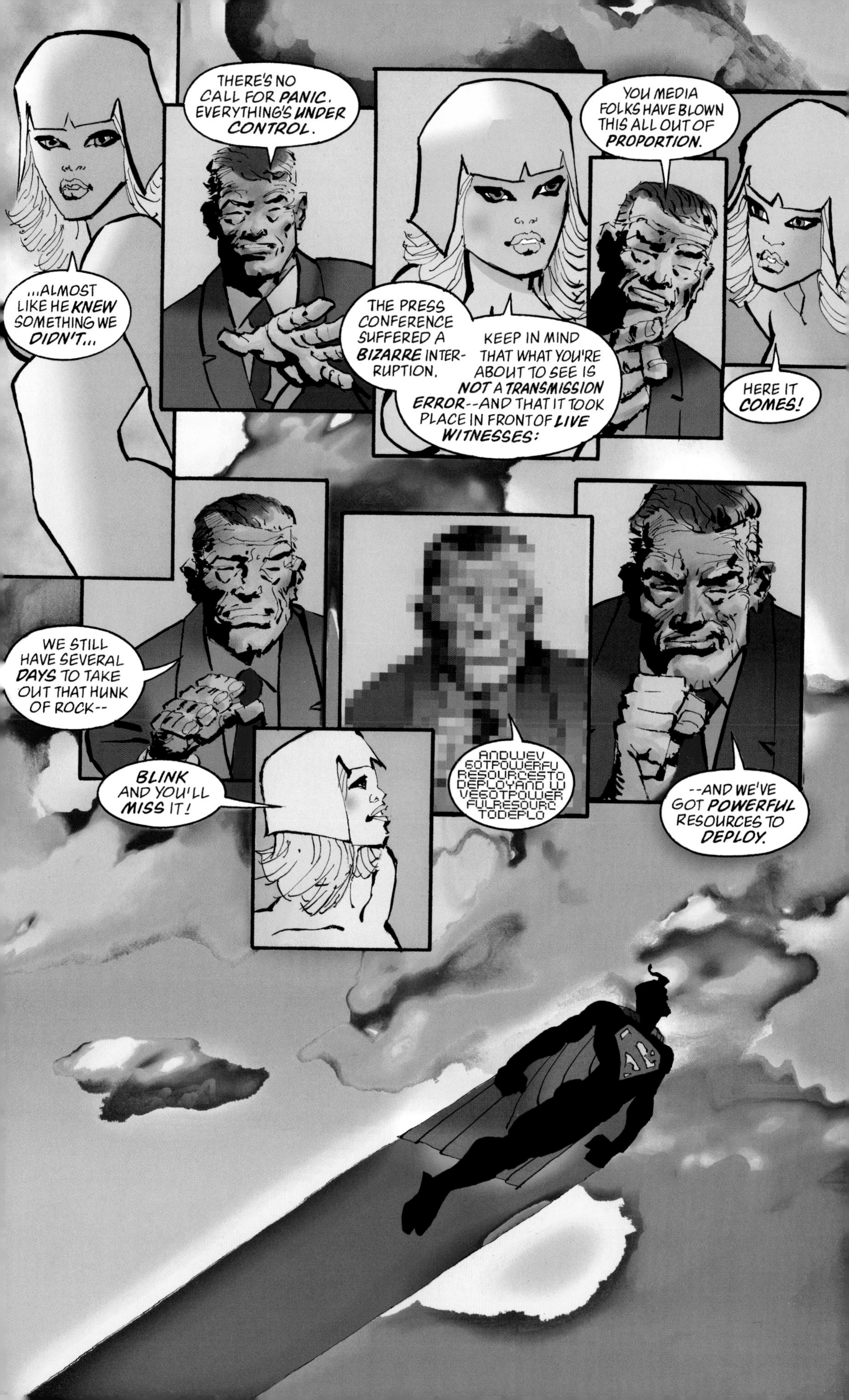

...ALMOST LIKE HE KNEW SOMETHING WE DIDN'T...
THERE'S NO CALL FOR PANIC. EVERYTHING'S UNDER CONTROL.
THE PRESS CONFERENCE SUFFERED A BIZARRE INTERRUPTION.
KEEP IN MIND THAT WHAT YOU'RE ABOUT TO SEE IS NOT A TRANSMISSION ERROR--AND THAT IT TOOK PLACE IN FRONT OF LIVE WITNESSES:
YOU MEDIA FOLKS HAVE BLOWN THIS ALL OUT OF PROPORTION.
HERE IT COMES!
WE STILL HAVE SEVERAL DAYS TO TAKE OUT THAT HUNK OF ROCK--
BLINK AND YOU'LL MISS IT!
ANDWEV GOTPOWERFU RESOURCESTO DEPLOYAND W VEGOTPOWER FULRESOURC TODEPLO
--AND WE'VE GOT POWERFUL RESOURCES TO DEPLOY.

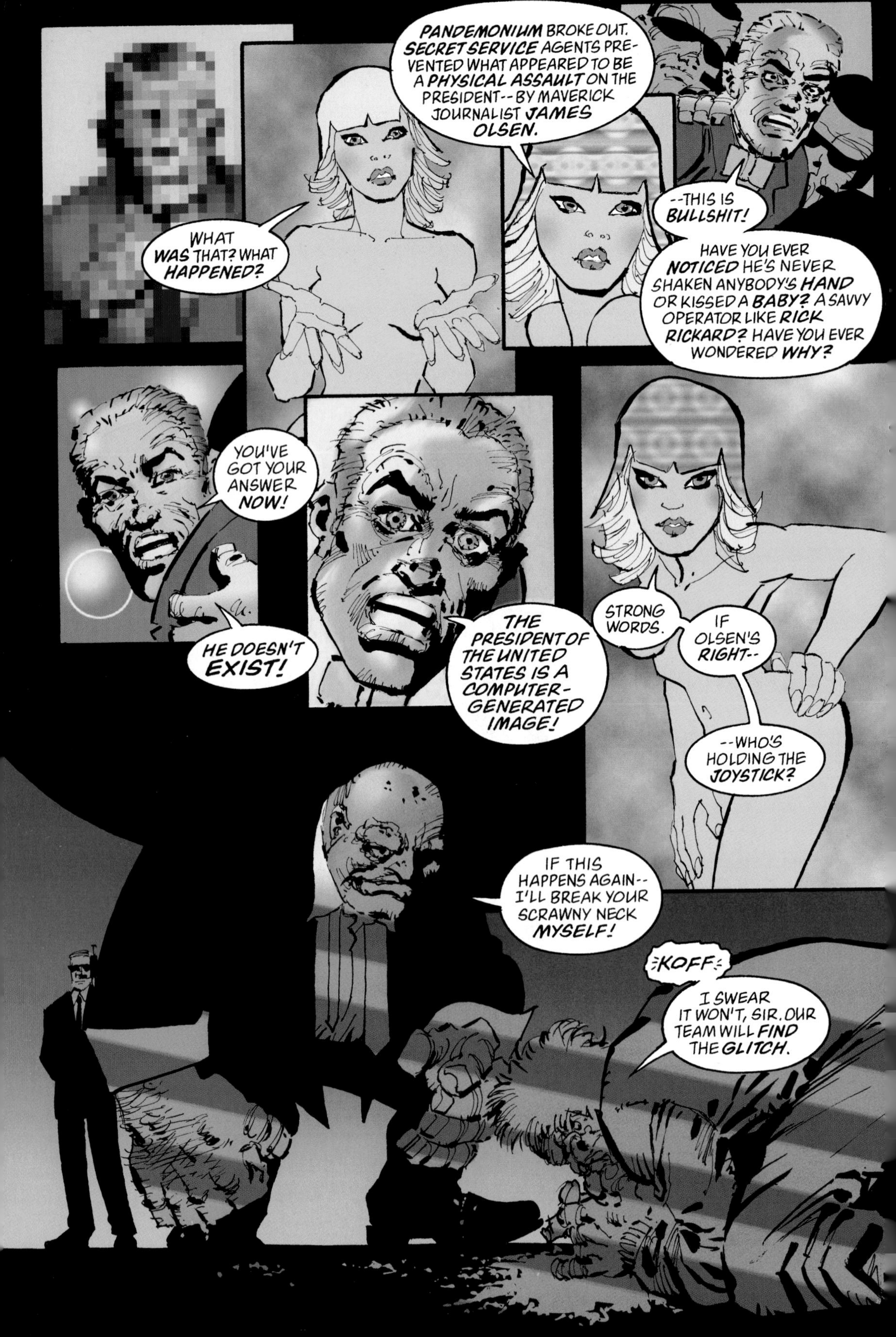
PANDEMONIUM BROKE OUT. SECRET SERVICE AGENTS PREVENTED WHAT APPEARED TO BE A PHYSICAL ASSAULT ON THE PRESIDENT--BY MAVERICK JOURNALIST JAMES OLSEN.
WHAT WAS THAT? WHAT HAPPENED?
--THIS IS BULLSHIT!
HAVE YOU EVER NOTICED HE'S NEVER SHAKEN ANYBODY'S HAND OR KISSED A BABY? A SAVVY OPERATOR LIKE RICK RICKARD? HAVE YOU EVER WONDERED WHY?
YOU'VE GOT YOUR ANSWER NOW!
HE DOESN'T EXIST!
THE PRESIDENT OF THE UNITED STATES IS A COMPUTER-GENERATED IMAGE!
STRONG WORDS.
IF OLSEN'S RIGHT--
--WHO'S HOLDING THE JOYSTICK?
IF THIS HAPPENS AGAIN--I'LL BREAK YOUR SCRAWNY NECK MYSELF!
KOFF
I SWEAR IT WON'T, SIR. OUR TEAM WILL FIND THE GLITCH.

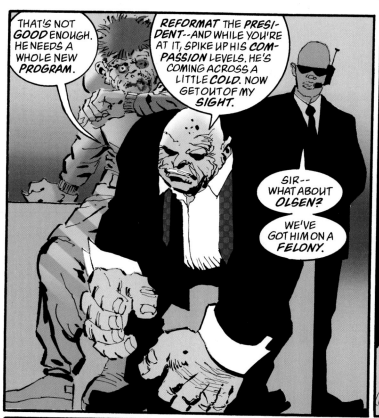

THAT'S NOT **GOOD** ENOUGH. HE NEEDS A WHOLE NEW **PROGRAM**.

REFORMAT THE PRESIDENT--AND WHILE YOU'RE AT IT, SPIKE UP HIS **COMPASSION** LEVELS. HE'S COMING ACROSS A LITTLE **COLD**. NOW GET OUT OF MY **SIGHT**.

SIR-- WHAT ABOUT **OLSEN?**

WE'VE GOT HIM ON A **FELONY**.

RELEASE HIM.

FREEDOM OF **SPEECH** IS A **WONDERFUL** THING-- SO LONG AS NOBODY'S **LISTENING**.

--SO LONG AS NOBODY'S **LISTENING**.

The world spins MAD.

The PEOPLE are so INTOXICATED by LUXURY they have FORGOTTEN everything that makes us more than HOUSE PETS.

REASON. TRUTH. JUSTICE.

FREEDOM.

The HUMAN SPIRIT is a shattered pane of GLASS-- wrapped in soft VELVET and soaked in sugary POISON.

EVIL has SEDUCED mankind. And MANKIND has shown all the CHASTITY of a three-dollar WHORE.

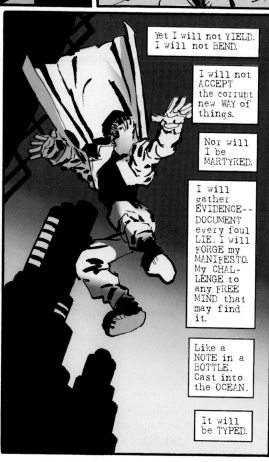

Yet I will not YIELD. I will not BEND.

I will not ACCEPT the corrupt new WAY of things.

Nor will I be MARTYRED.

I will gather EVIDENCE-- DOCUMENT every foul LIE. I will FORGE my MANIFESTO. My CHALLENGE to any FREE MIND that may find it.

Like a NOTE in a BOTTLE. Cast into the OCEAN.

It will be TYPED.

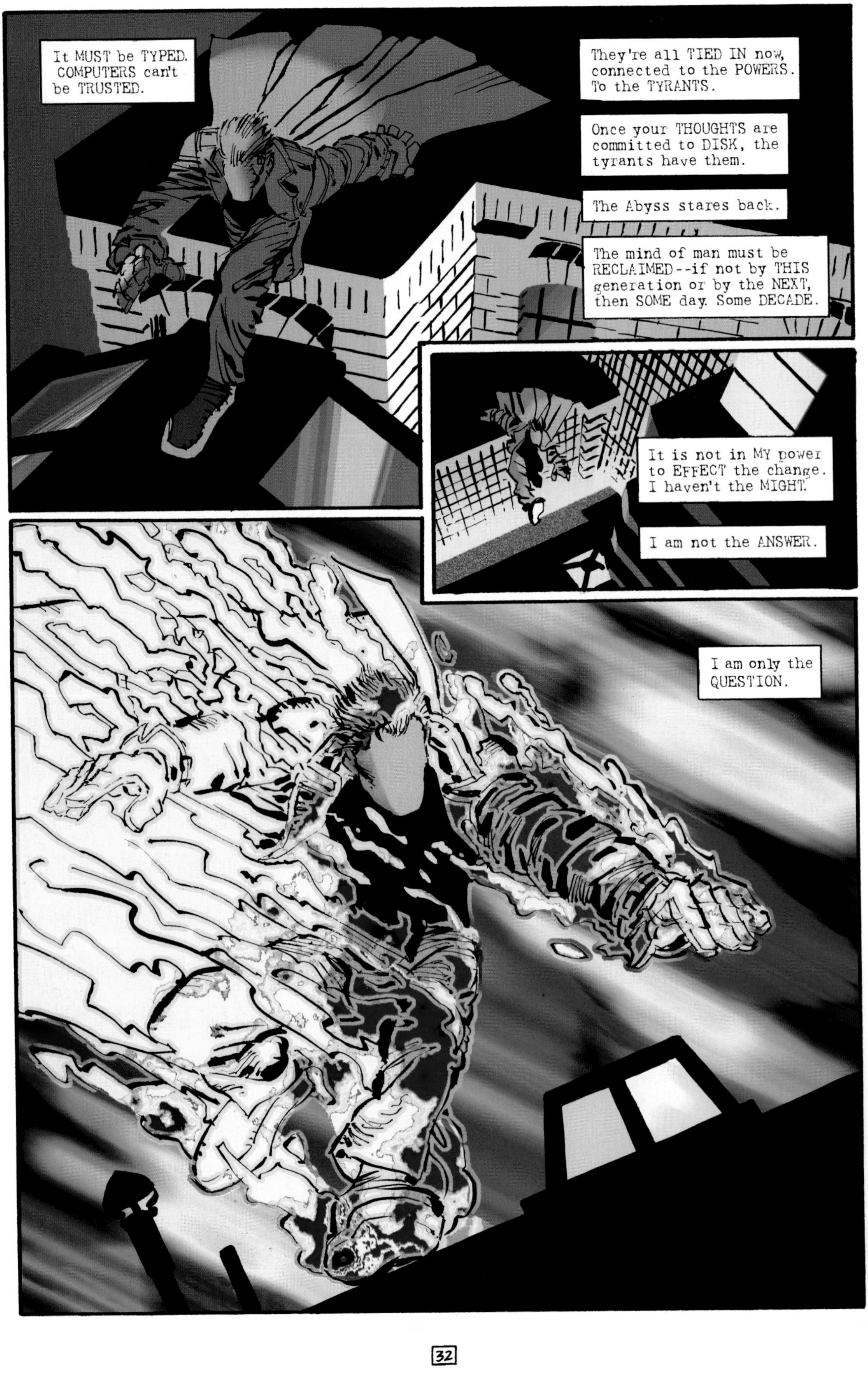
It MUST be TYPED. COMPUTERS can't be TRUSTED.
They're all TIED IN now, connected to the POWERS. To the TYRANTS.
Once your THOUGHTS are committed to DISK, the tyrants have them.
The Abyss stares back.
The mind of man must be RECLAIMED--if not by THIS generation or by the NEXT, then SOME day. Some DECADE.
It is not in MY power to EFFECT the change. I haven't the MIGHT.
I am not the ANSWER.
I am only the QUESTION.

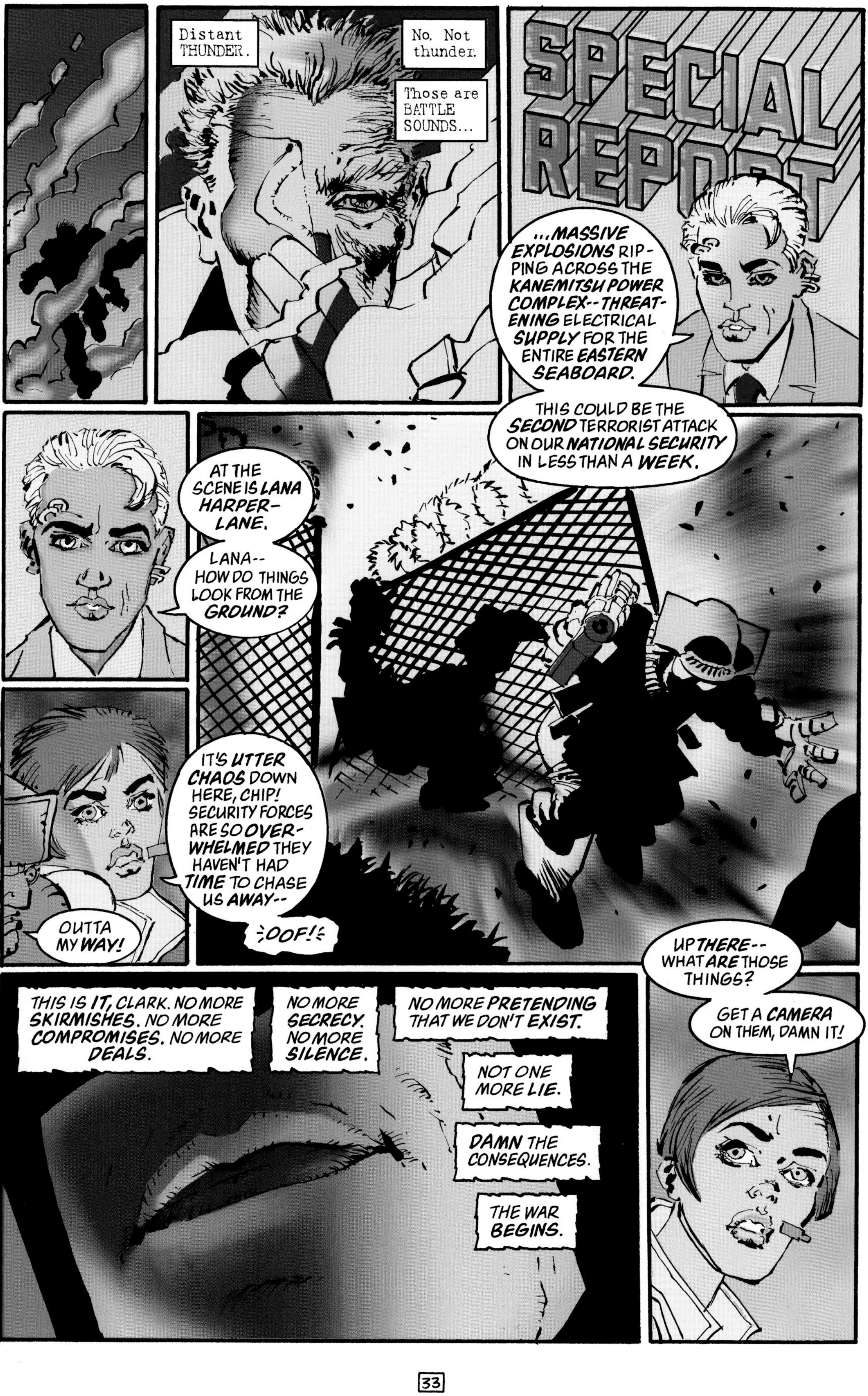

Distant THUNDER.
No. Not thunder.
Those are BATTLE SOUNDS...
SPECIAL REPORT
...MASSIVE EXPLOSIONS RIPPING ACROSS THE KANEMITSU POWER COMPLEX--THREATENING ELECTRICAL SUPPLY FOR THE ENTIRE EASTERN SEABOARD.
THIS COULD BE THE SECOND TERRORIST ATTACK ON OUR NATIONAL SECURITY IN LESS THAN A WEEK.
AT THE SCENE IS LANA HARPER-LANE.
LANA-- HOW DO THINGS LOOK FROM THE GROUND?
IT'S UTTER CHAOS DOWN HERE, CHIP! SECURITY FORCES ARE SO OVERWHELMED THEY HAVEN'T HAD TIME TO CHASE US AWAY--
OUTTA MY WAY!
OOF!
UP THERE-- WHAT ARE THOSE THINGS?
GET A CAMERA ON THEM, DAMN IT!
THIS IS IT, CLARK. NO MORE SKIRMISHES. NO MORE COMPROMISES. NO MORE DEALS.
NO MORE SECRECY. NO MORE SILENCE.
NO MORE PRETENDING THAT WE DON'T EXIST.
NOT ONE MORE LIE.
DAMN THE CONSEQUENCES.
THE WAR BEGINS.

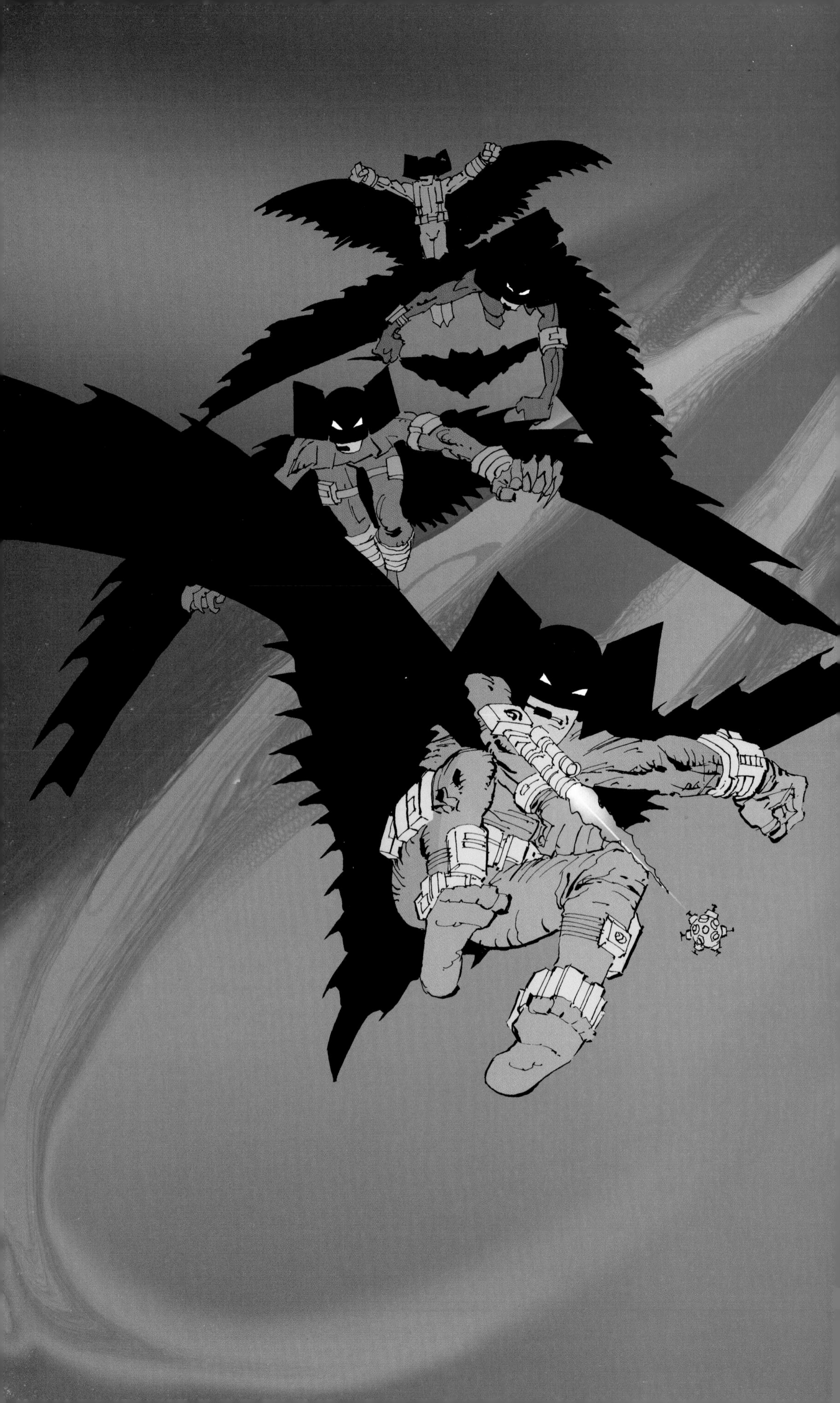

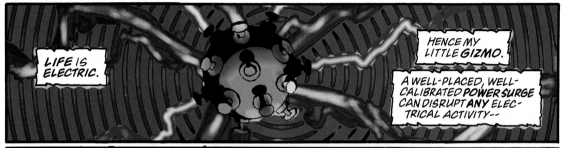

LIFE IS ELECTRIC.

HENCE MY LITTLE *GIZMO.*

A WELL-PLACED, WELL-CALIBRATED *POWER SURGE* CAN DISRUPT *ANY* ELECTRICAL ACTIVITY--

--EVEN THE *HUMAN NERVOUS SYSTEM.*

MY LITTLE *GIZMO.* IT WORKS BETTER THAN *NERVE GAS.*

TOO BAD IT DOESN'T WORK ON *KRYPTONIANS.* BUT I'VE GOT SOME *OTHER* SWEET TRICKS PLANNED FOR *YOU,* CLARK...

TAK *TAK*

THAT WAS THE *EASY* PART, *BATBOYS!* NOW *BEAT FEET!* WE'RE GOING *IN!*

HERB-- THAT *CANNON* UP AHEAD-- CHANGE ITS *MIND.*

SURE THING, COMMANDER! CONFIDENCE IS HIGH!

INTRUDER. TARGETING *PROTON BLAST.*

SENDING *COMMAND SIGNAL.*

VOOP

POOM

COMMAND SIGNAL RECEIVED.

ENJOY YOUR STAY.

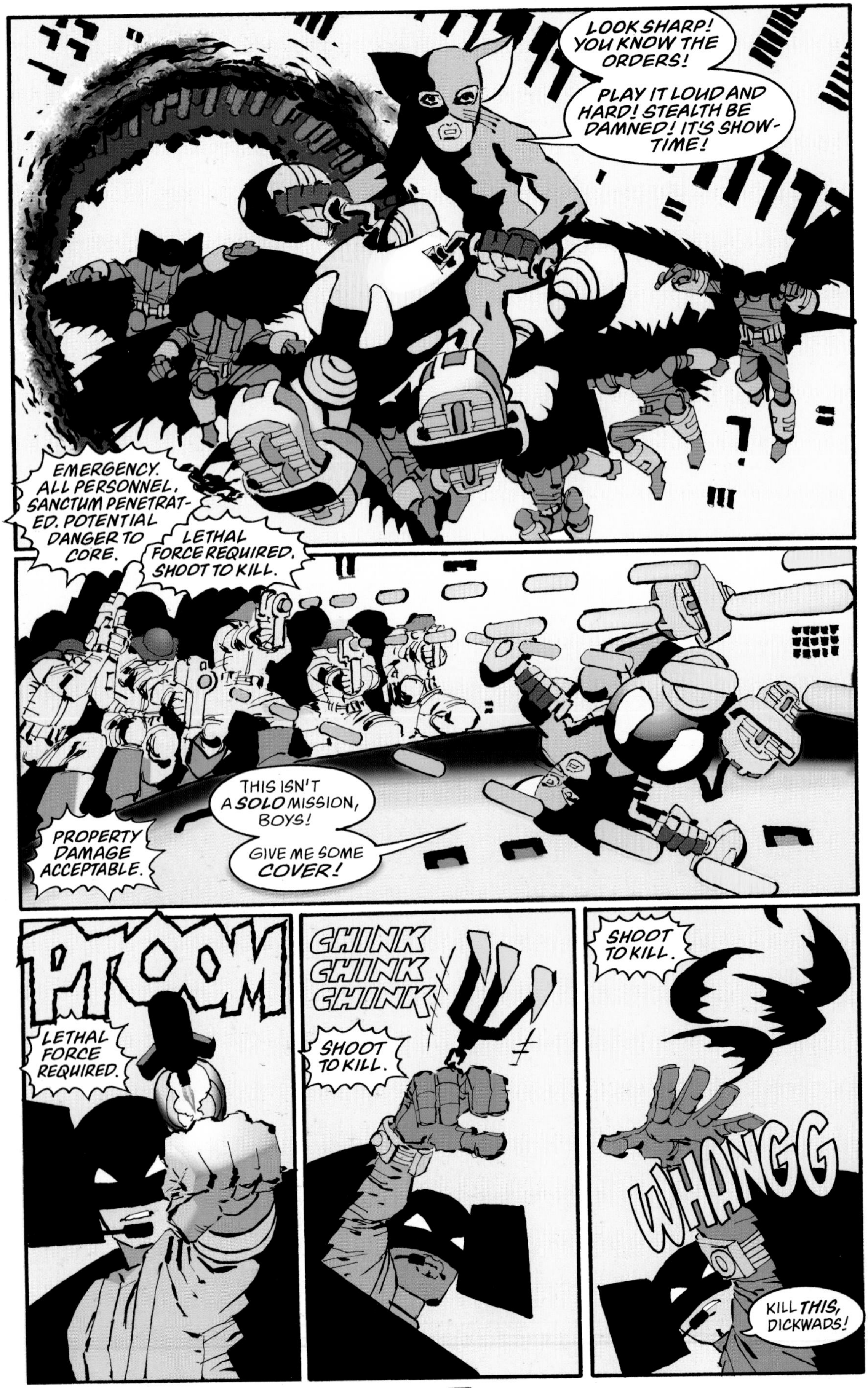
LOOK SHARP! YOU KNOW THE ORDERS!
PLAY IT LOUD AND HARD! STEALTH BE DAMNED! IT'S SHOW-TIME!
EMERGENCY. ALL PERSONNEL. SANCTUM PENETRATED. POTENTIAL DANGER TO CORE.
LETHAL FORCE REQUIRED. SHOOT TO KILL.
PROPERTY DAMAGE ACCEPTABLE.
THIS ISN'T A SOLO MISSION, BOYS!
GIVE ME SOME COVER!
PTOOM
LETHAL FORCE REQUIRED.
CHINK CHINK CHINK
SHOOT TO KILL.
SHOOT TO KILL.
WHANGG
KILL THIS, DICKWADS!

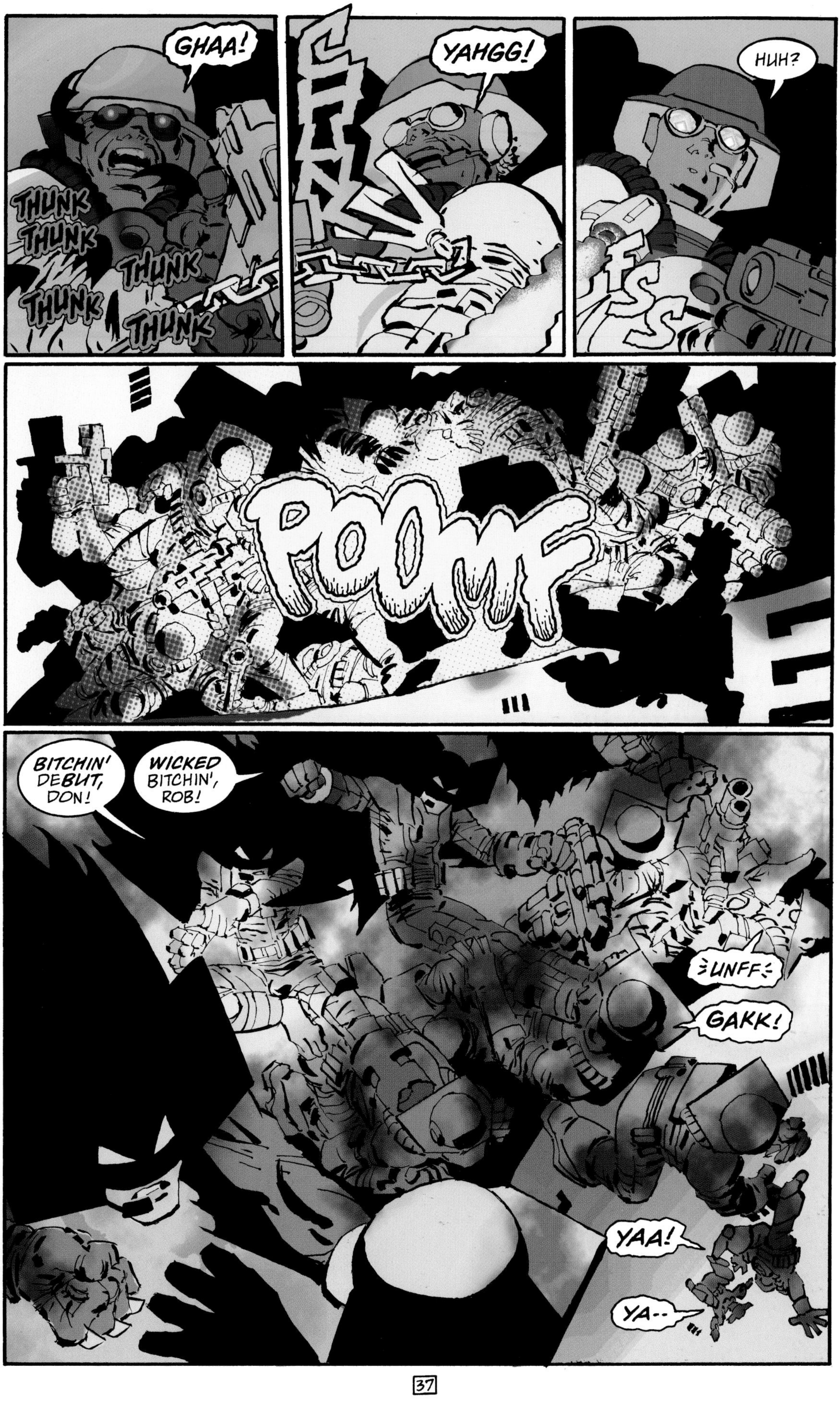
GHAA!
THUNK
THUNK
THUNK
THUNK
THUNK
YAHGG!
HUH?
FSS
POOMF
BITCHIN' DEBUT, DON!
WICKED BITCHIN', ROB!
UNFF
GAKK!
YAA!
YA--

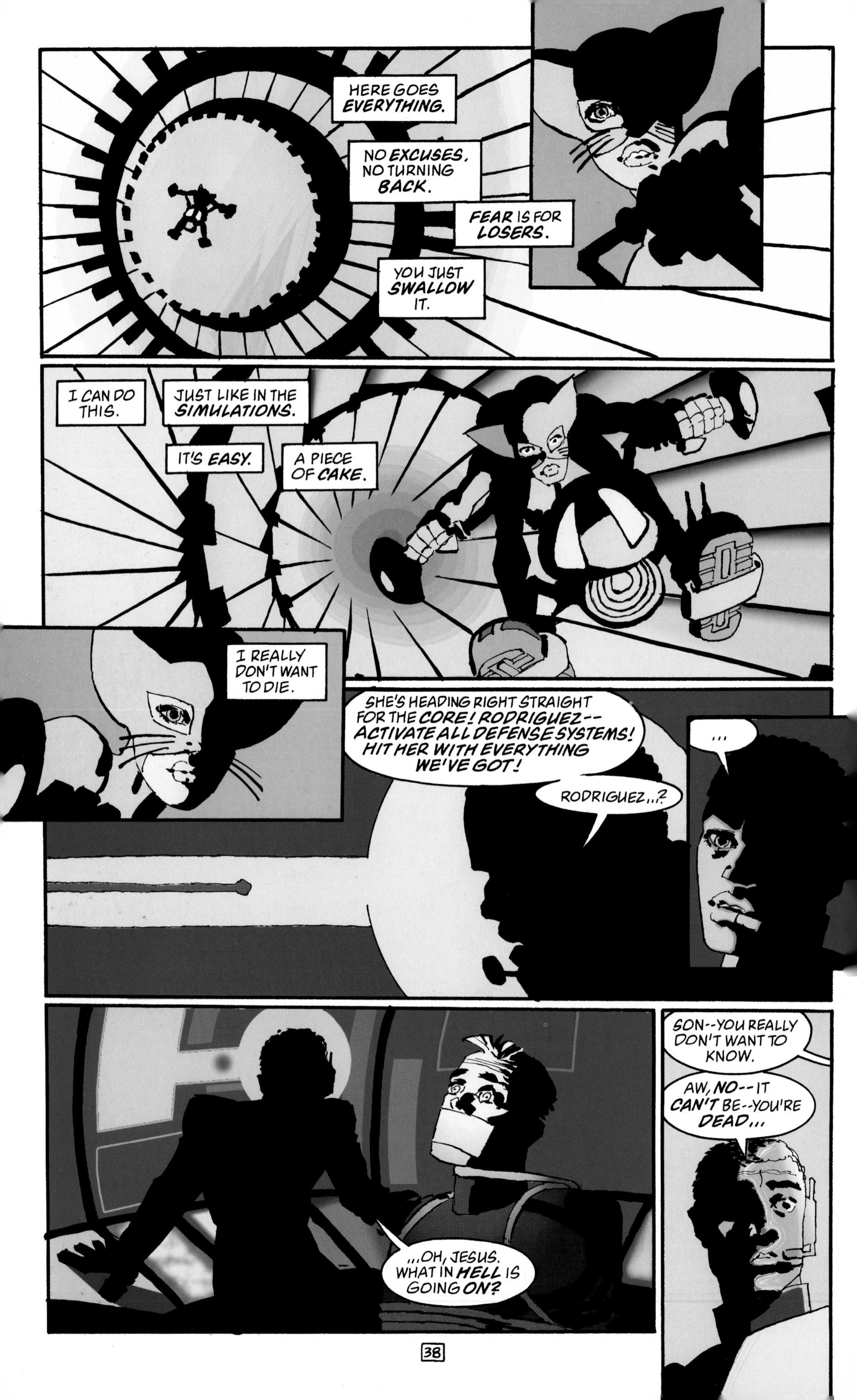
HERE GOES EVERYTHING.
NO EXCUSES. NO TURNING BACK.
FEAR IS FOR LOSERS.
YOU JUST SWALLOW IT.
I CAN DO THIS.
JUST LIKE IN THE SIMULATIONS.
IT'S EASY.
A PIECE OF CAKE.
I REALLY DON'T WANT TO DIE.
SHE'S HEADING RIGHT STRAIGHT FOR THE CORE! RODRIGUEZ-- ACTIVATE ALL DEFENSE SYSTEMS! HIT HER WITH EVERYTHING WE'VE GOT!
...
RODRIGUEZ...?
...OH, JESUS. WHAT IN HELL IS GOING ON?
SON--YOU REALLY DON'T WANT TO KNOW.
AW, NO--IT CAN'T BE--YOU'RE DEAD...

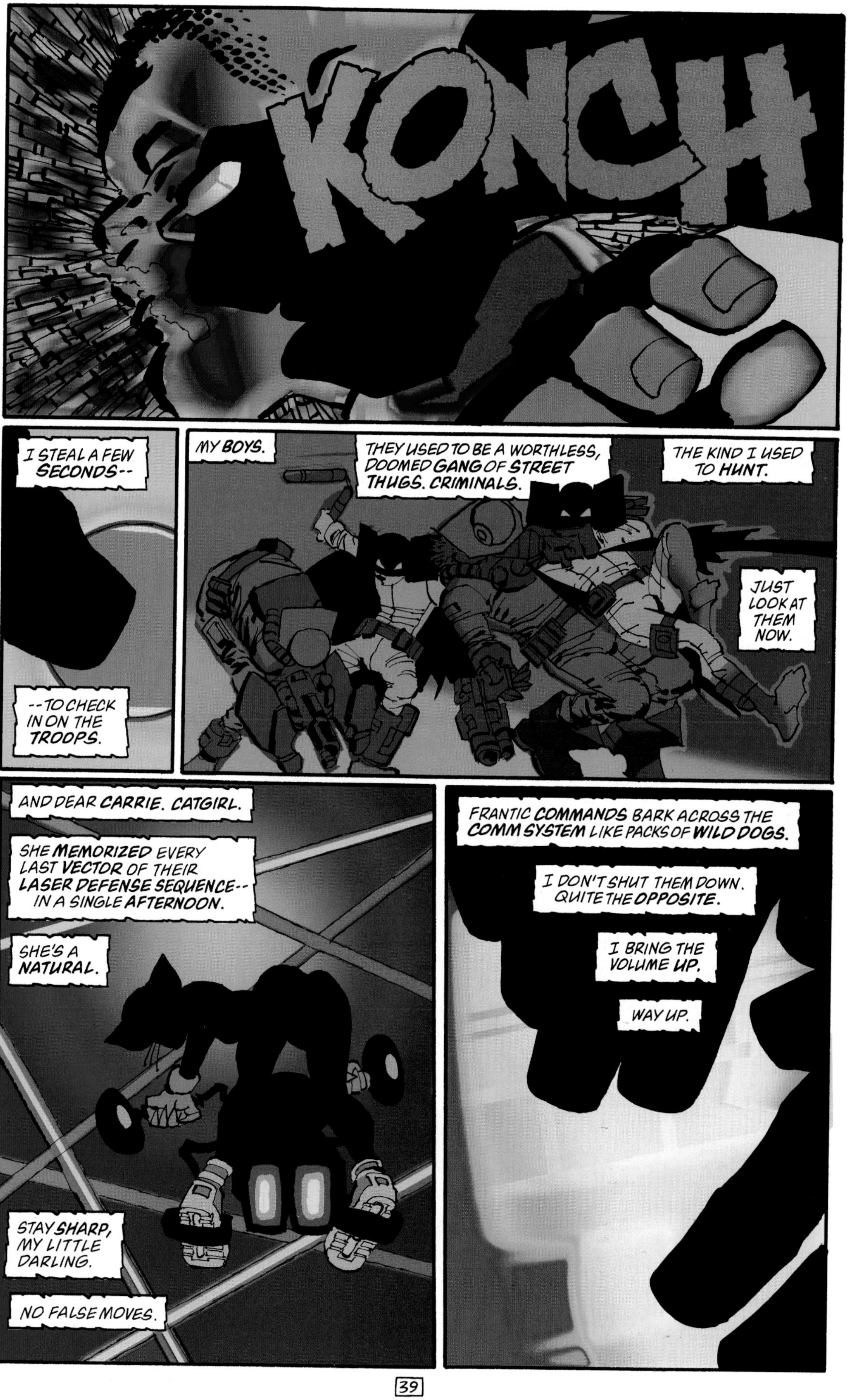

KONCH
I STEAL A FEW SECONDS--
--TO CHECK IN ON THE TROOPS.
MY BOYS.
THEY USED TO BE A WORTHLESS, DOOMED GANG OF STREET THUGS. CRIMINALS.
THE KIND I USED TO HUNT.
JUST LOOK AT THEM NOW.
AND DEAR CARRIE. CATGIRL.
SHE MEMORIZED EVERY LAST VECTOR OF THEIR LASER DEFENSE SEQUENCE-- IN A SINGLE AFTERNOON.
SHE'S A NATURAL.
STAY SHARP, MY LITTLE DARLING.
NO FALSE MOVES.
FRANTIC COMMANDS BARK ACROSS THE COMM SYSTEM LIKE PACKS OF WILD DOGS.
I DON'T SHUT THEM DOWN. QUITE THE OPPOSITE.
I BRING THE VOLUME UP.
WAY UP.

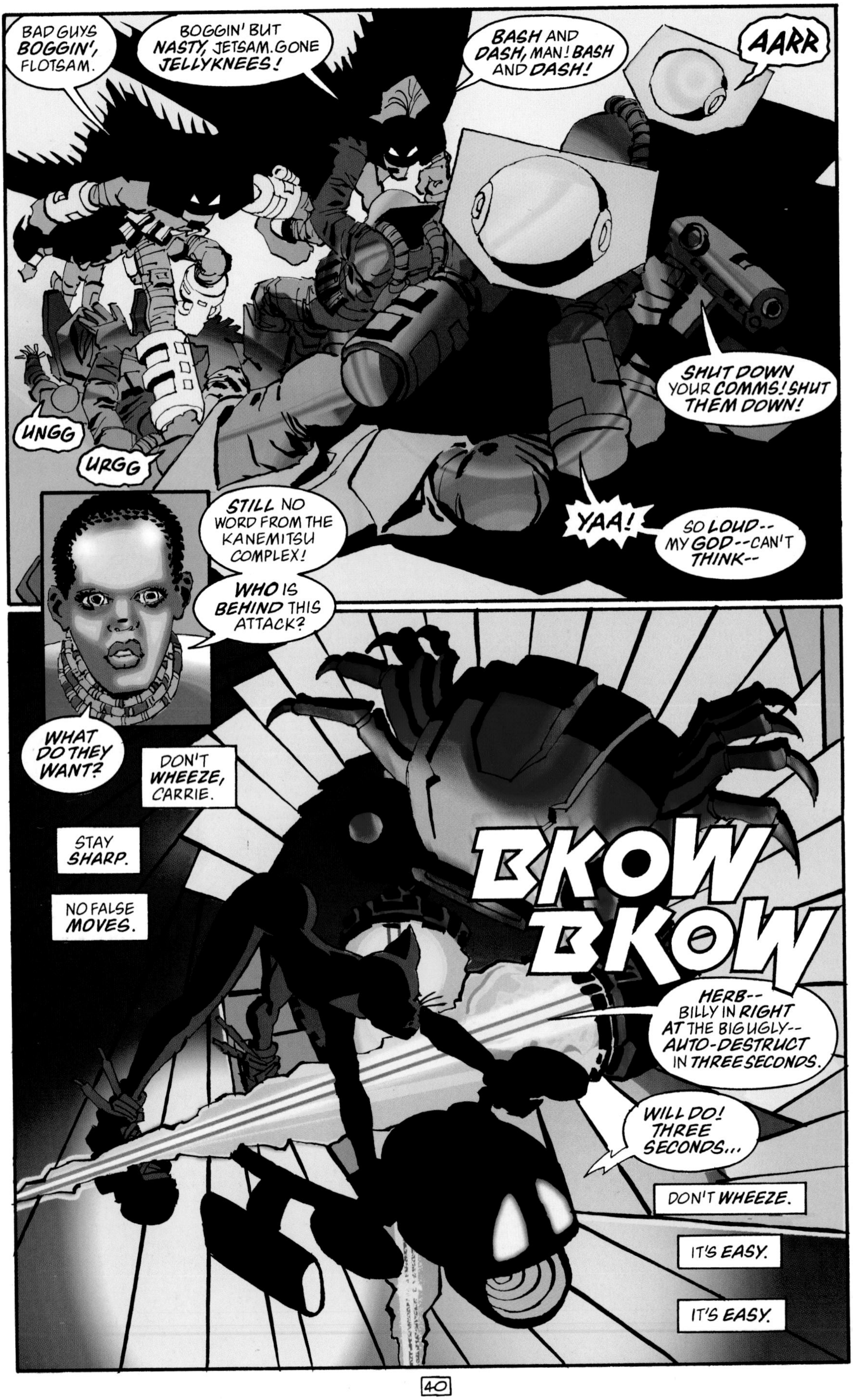
BAD GUYS BOGGIN', FLOTSAM.
BOGGIN' BUT NASTY, JETSAM. GONE JELLYKNEES!
BASH AND DASH, MAN! BASH AND DASH!
AARR
SHUT DOWN YOUR COMMS! SHUT THEM DOWN!
UNGG
URGG
YAA!
SO LOUD-- MY GOD--CAN'T THINK--
STILL NO WORD FROM THE KANEMITSU COMPLEX!
WHO IS BEHIND THIS ATTACK?
WHAT DO THEY WANT?
DON'T WHEEZE, CARRIE.
STAY SHARP.
NO FALSE MOVES.
BKOW BKOW
HERB-- BILLY IN RIGHT AT THE BIG UGLY-- AUTO-DESTRUCT IN THREE SECONDS.
WILL DO! THREE SECONDS...
DON'T WHEEZE.
IT'S EASY.
IT'S EASY.

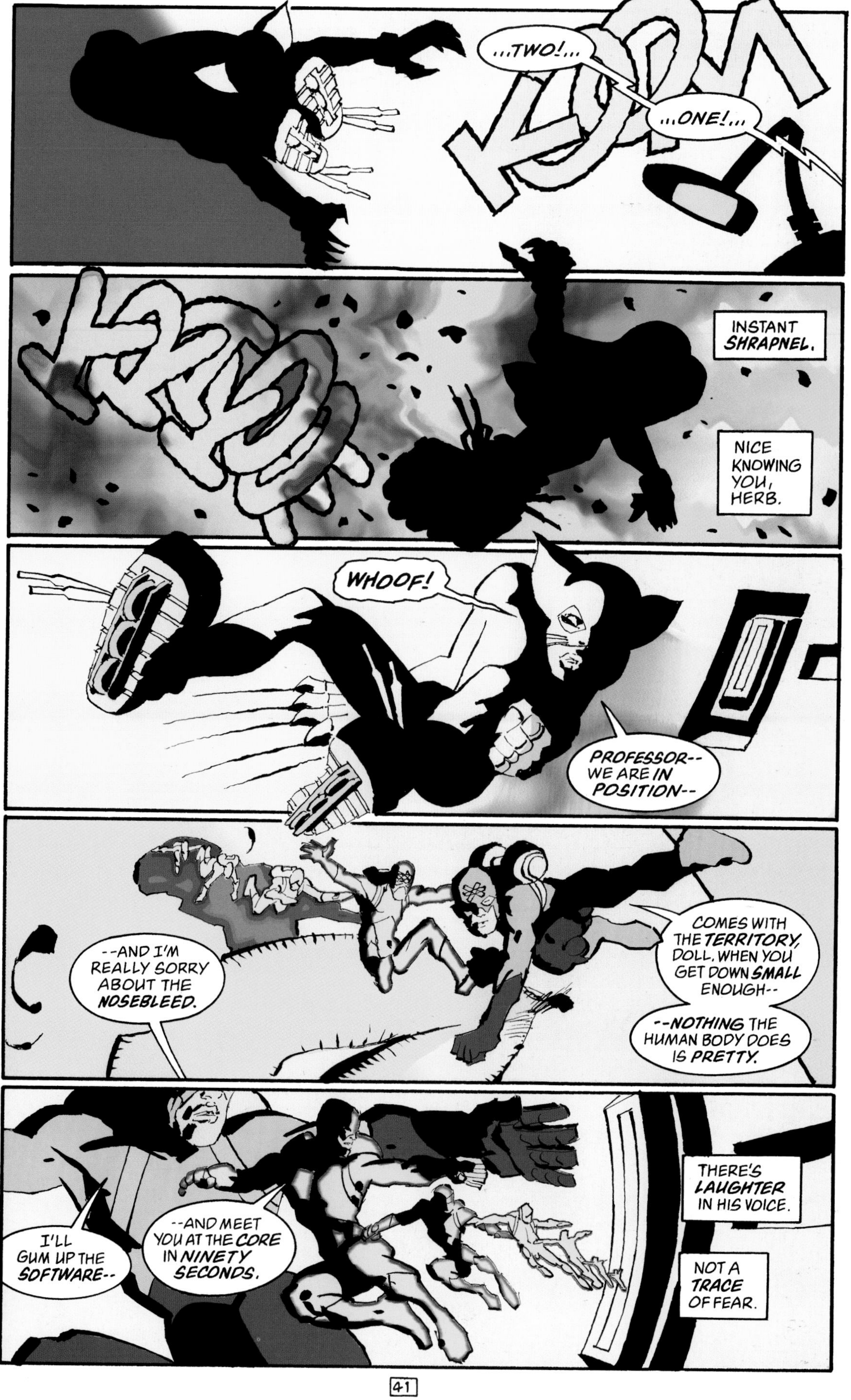
...TWO!...
...ONE!...
INSTANT SHRAPNEL.
NICE KNOWING YOU, HERB.
WHOOF!
PROFESSOR-- WE ARE IN POSITION--
--AND I'M REALLY SORRY ABOUT THE NOSEBLEED.
COMES WITH THE TERRITORY, DOLL, WHEN YOU GET DOWN SMALL ENOUGH--
--NOTHING THE HUMAN BODY DOES IS PRETTY.
I'LL GUM UP THE SOFTWARE--
--AND MEET YOU AT THE CORE IN NINETY SECONDS.
THERE'S LAUGHTER IN HIS VOICE.
NOT A TRACE OF FEAR.

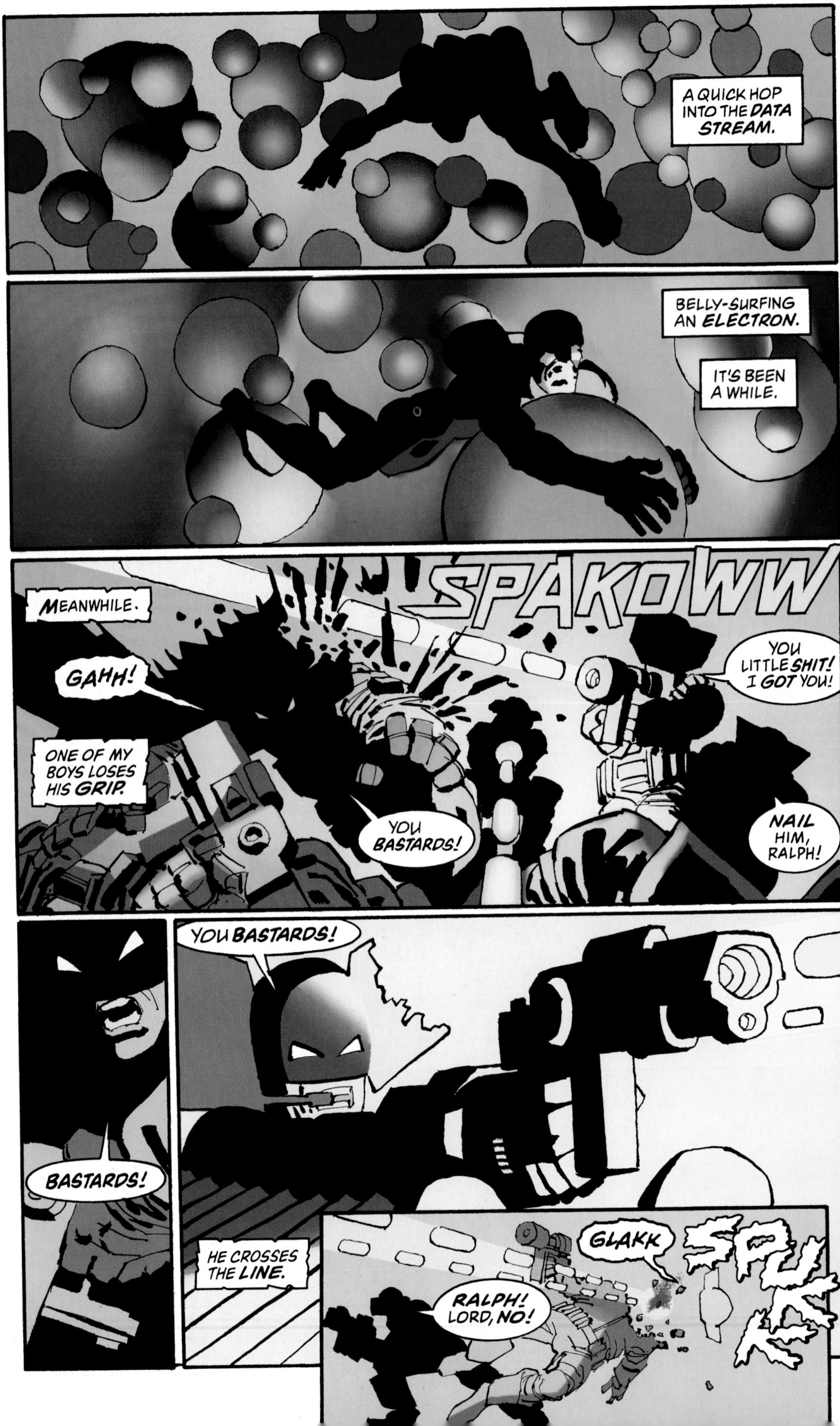
A QUICK HOP INTO THE DATA STREAM.
BELLY-SURFING AN ELECTRON.
IT'S BEEN A WHILE.
SPAKOWW
MEANWHILE.
GAHH!
YOU LITTLE SHIT! I GOT YOU!
ONE OF MY BOYS LOSES HIS GRIP.
YOU BASTARDS!
NAIL HIM, RALPH!
YOU BASTARDS!
BASTARDS!
HE CROSSES THE LINE.
GLAKK
SPUKK
RALPH! LORD, NO!

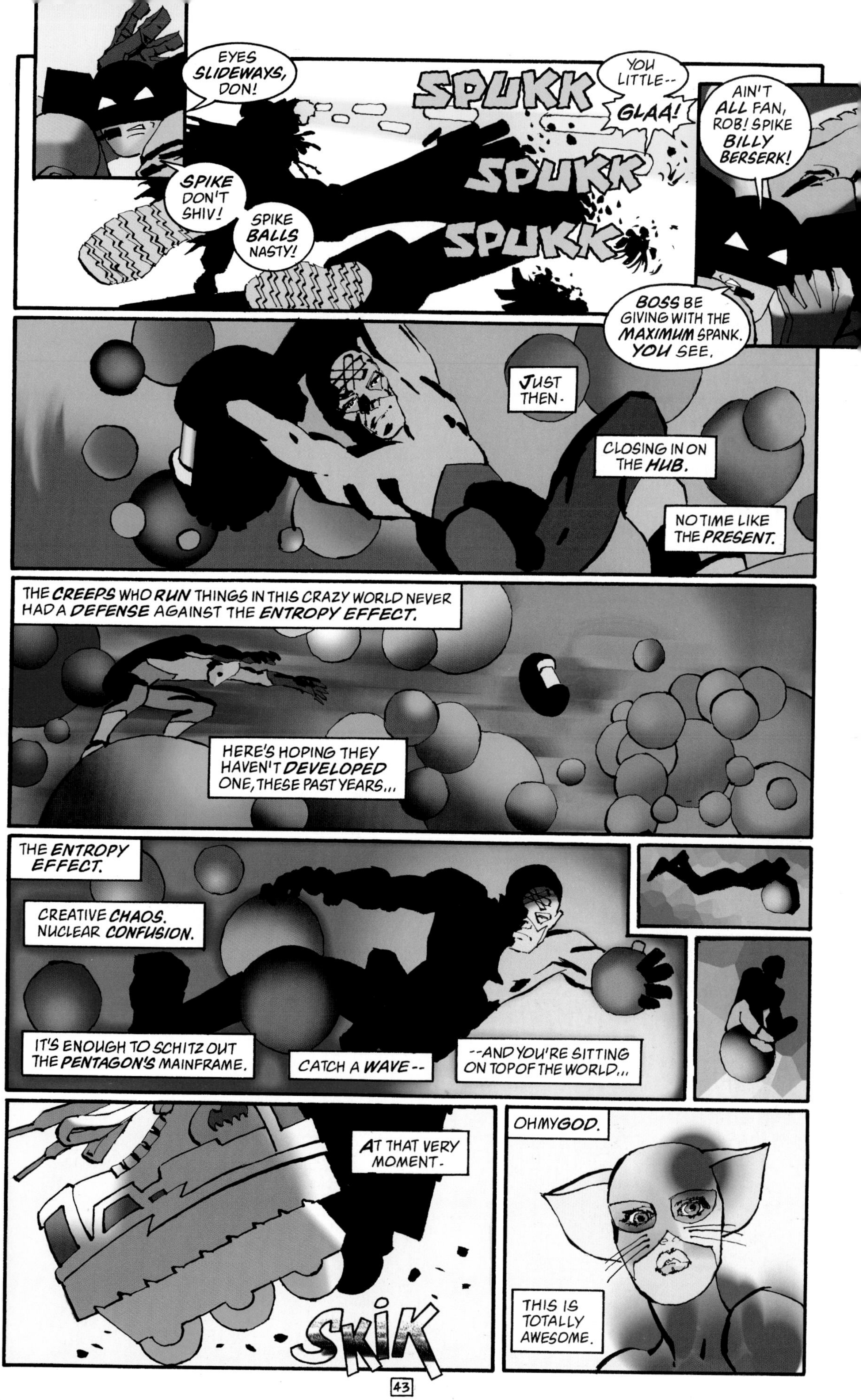
EYES SLIDEWAYS, DON!
SPIKE DON'T SHIV!
SPIKE BALLS NASTY!
SPUKK
YOU LITTLE--
GLAA!
SPUKK
SPUKK
AIN'T ALL FAN, ROB! SPIKE BILLY BERSERK!
BOSS BE GIVING WITH THE MAXIMUM SPANK. YOU SEE.
JUST THEN.
CLOSING IN ON THE HUB.
NO TIME LIKE THE PRESENT.
THE CREEPS WHO RUN THINGS IN THIS CRAZY WORLD NEVER HAD A DEFENSE AGAINST THE ENTROPY EFFECT.
HERE'S HOPING THEY HAVEN'T DEVELOPED ONE, THESE PAST YEARS...
THE ENTROPY EFFECT.
CREATIVE CHAOS. NUCLEAR CONFUSION.
IT'S ENOUGH TO SCHITZ OUT THE PENTAGON'S MAINFRAME.
CATCH A WAVE --
--AND YOU'RE SITTING ON TOP OF THE WORLD...
AT THAT VERY MOMENT.
SKIK
OHMYGOD.
THIS IS TOTALLY AWESOME.

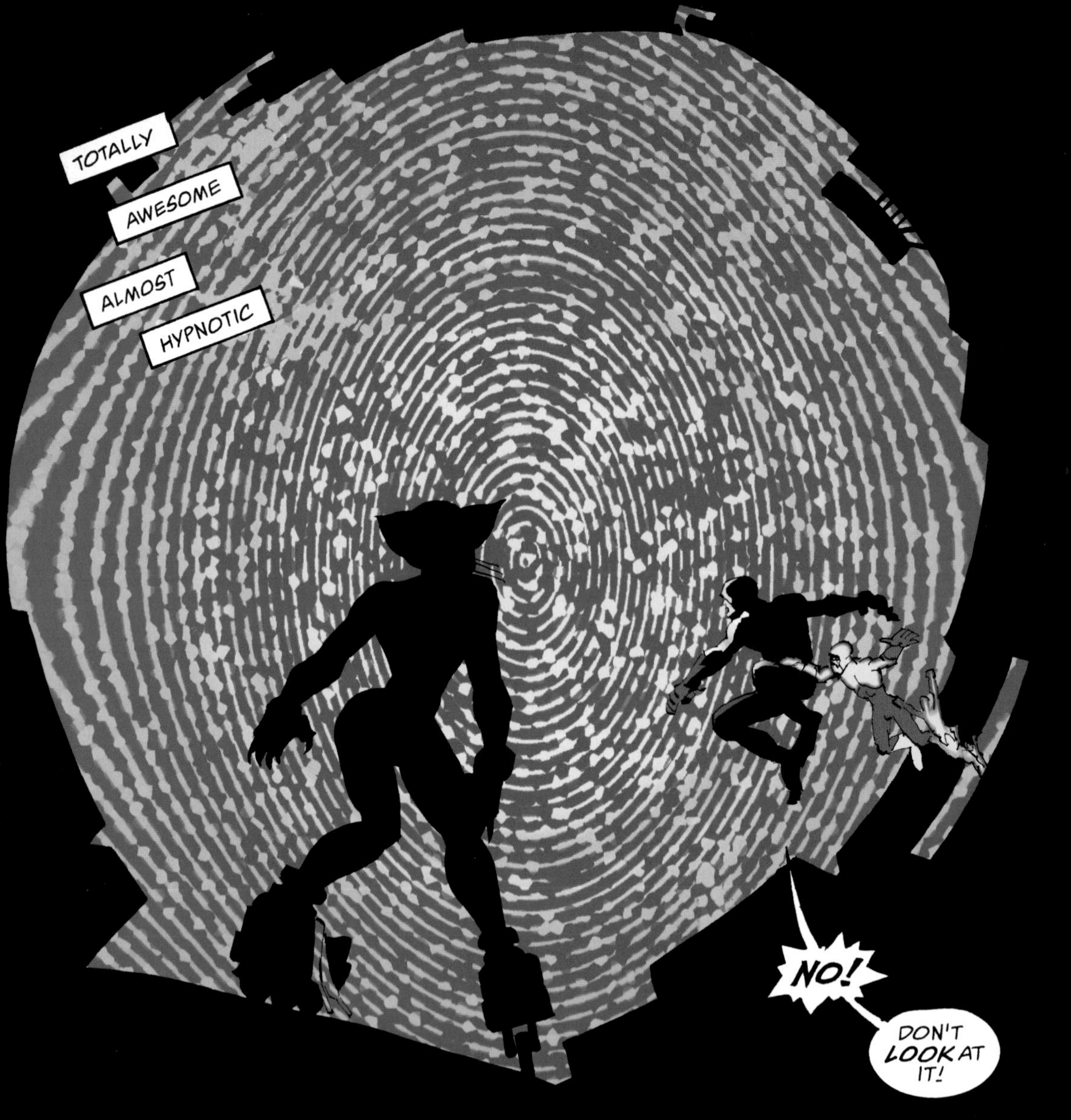
TOTALLY
AWESOME
ALMOST
HYPNOTIC
NO!
DON'T LOOK AT IT!

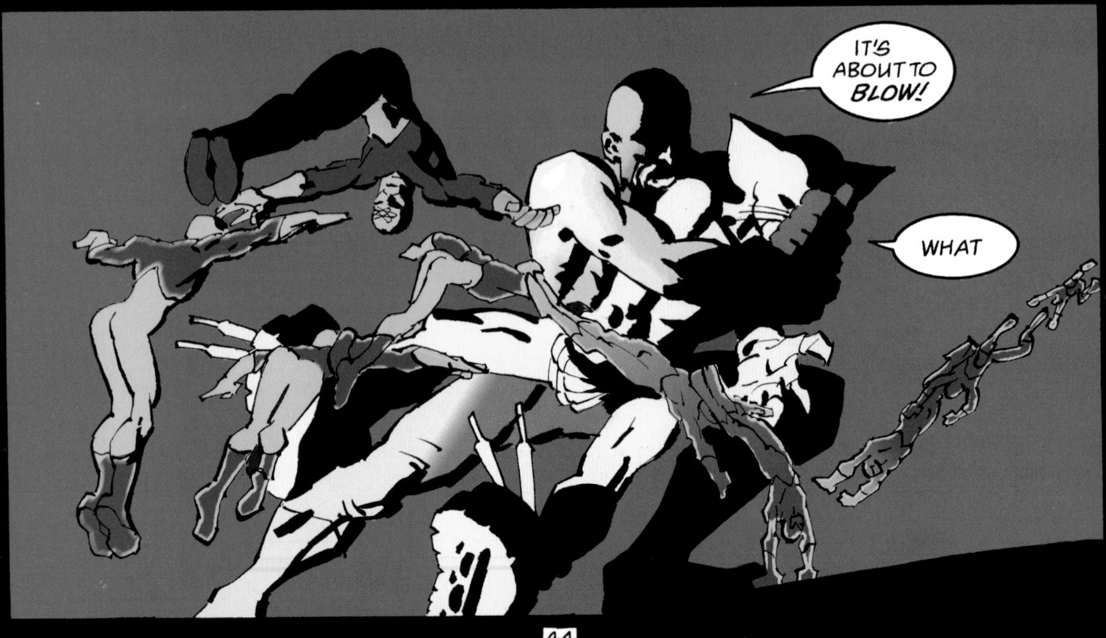
IT'S ABOUT TO BLOW!
WHAT

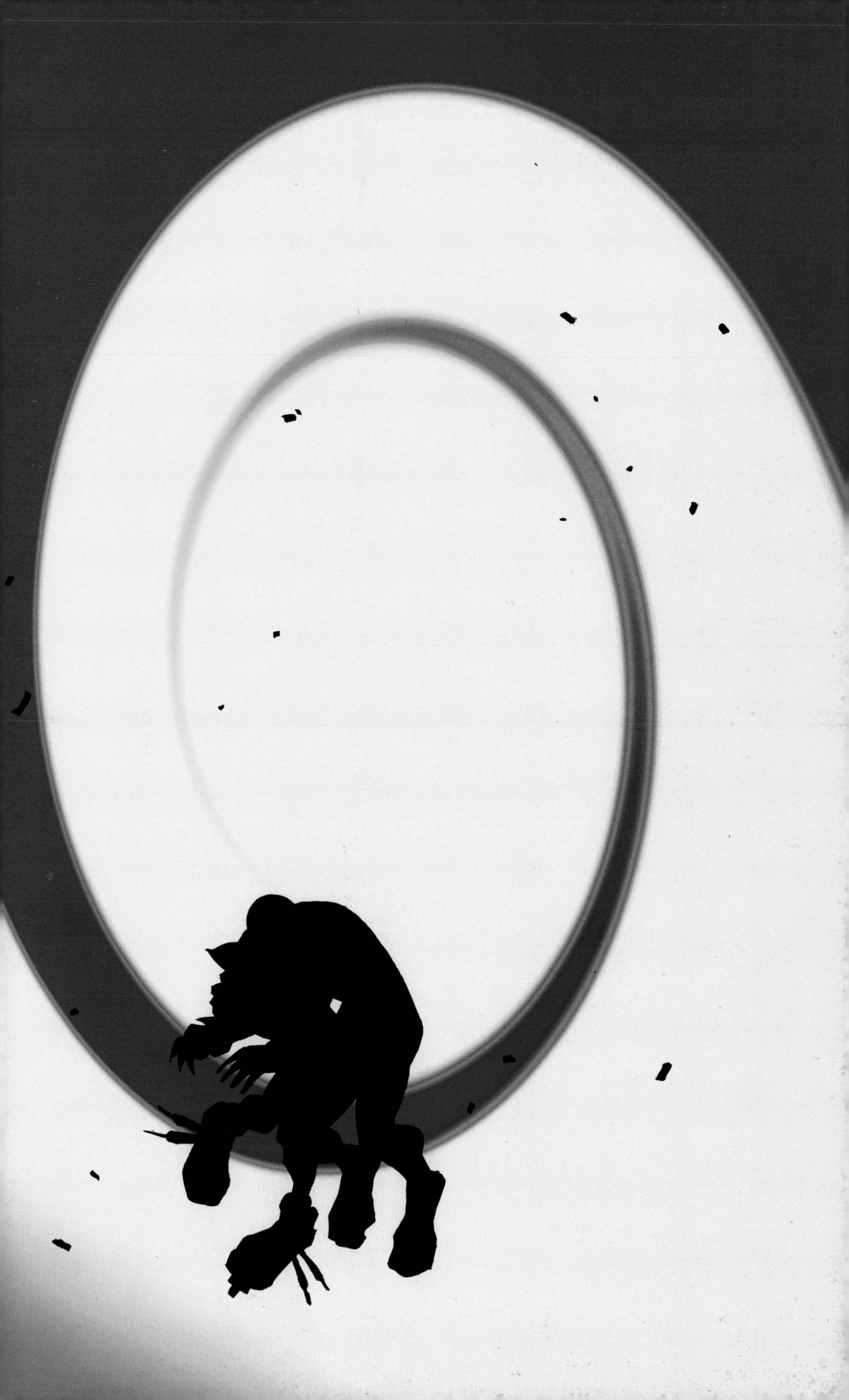

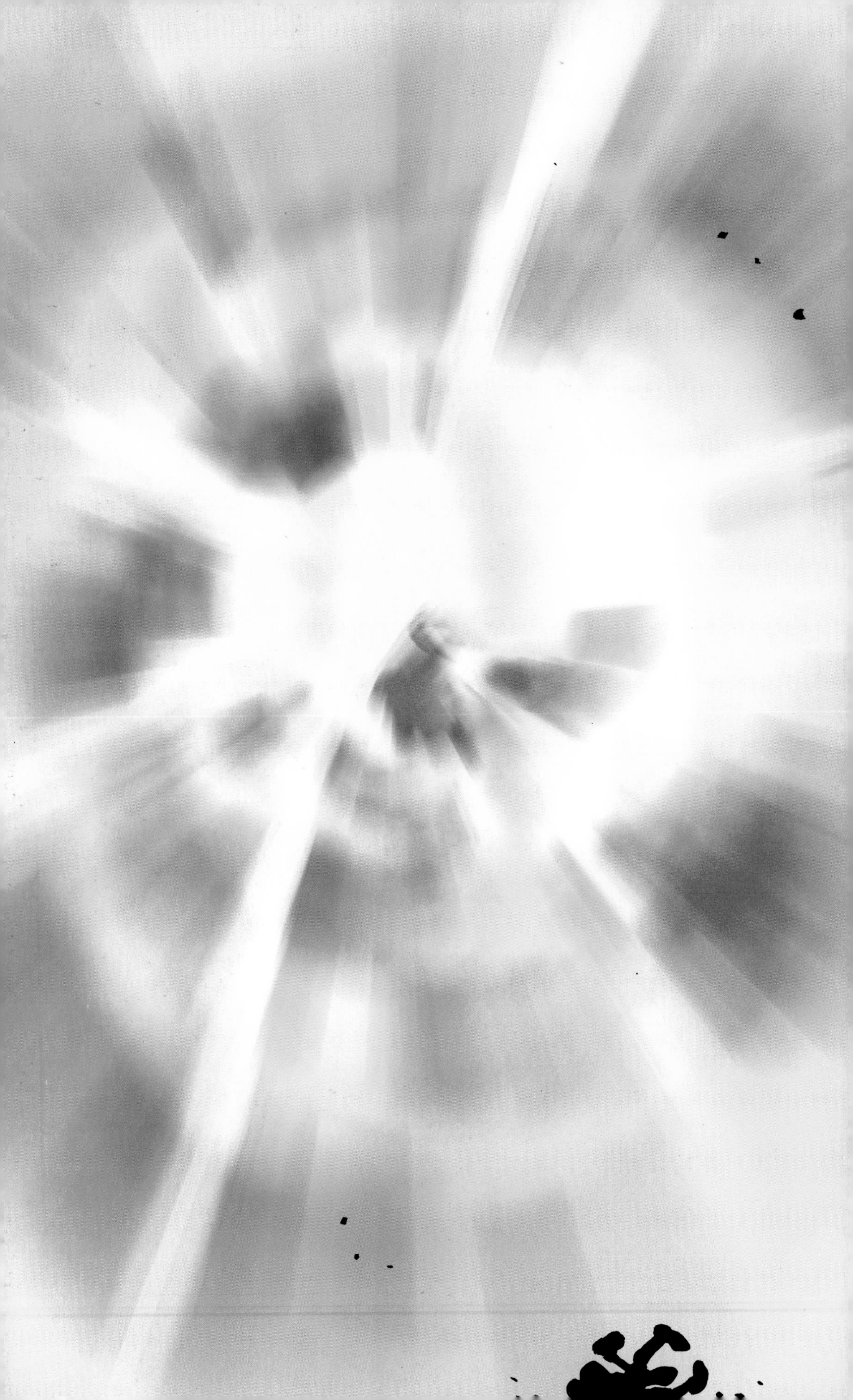

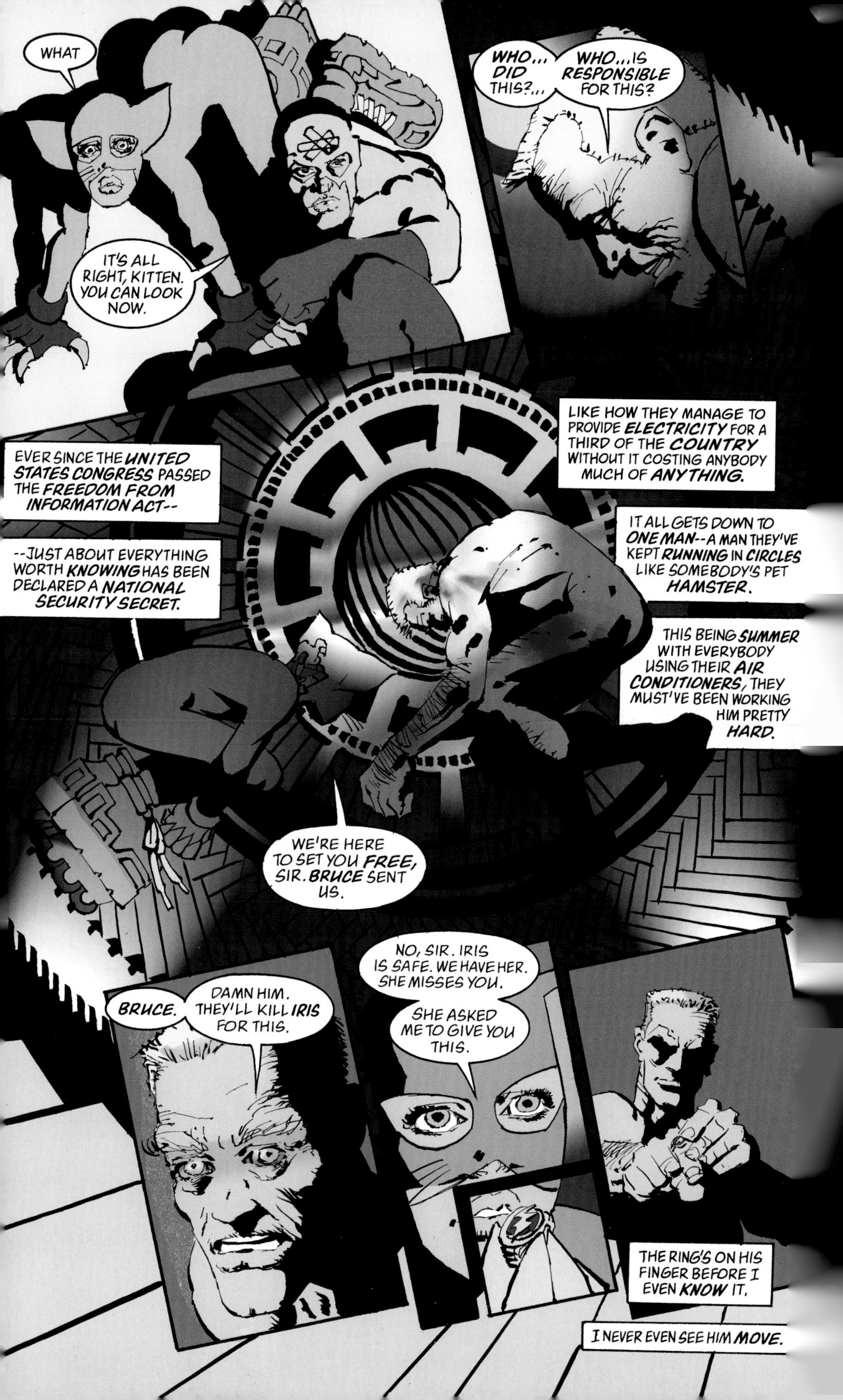
WHAT
IT'S ALL RIGHT, KITTEN. YOU CAN LOOK NOW.
WHO... DID THIS?...
WHO... IS RESPONSIBLE FOR THIS?
EVER SINCE THE UNITED STATES CONGRESS PASSED THE FREEDOM FROM INFORMATION ACT--
--JUST ABOUT EVERYTHING WORTH KNOWING HAS BEEN DECLARED A NATIONAL SECURITY SECRET.
LIKE HOW THEY MANAGE TO PROVIDE ELECTRICITY FOR A THIRD OF THE COUNTRY WITHOUT IT COSTING ANYBODY MUCH OF ANYTHING.
IT ALL GETS DOWN TO ONE MAN--A MAN THEY'VE KEPT RUNNING IN CIRCLES LIKE SOMEBODY'S PET HAMSTER.
THIS BEING SUMMER WITH EVERYBODY USING THEIR AIR CONDITIONERS, THEY MUST'VE BEEN WORKING HIM PRETTY HARD.
WE'RE HERE TO SET YOU FREE, SIR. BRUCE SENT US.
BRUCE.
DAMN HIM. THEY'LL KILL IRIS FOR THIS.
NO, SIR. IRIS IS SAFE. WE HAVE HER. SHE MISSES YOU.
SHE ASKED ME TO GIVE YOU THIS.
THE RING'S ON HIS FINGER BEFORE I EVEN KNOW IT.
I NEVER EVEN SEE HIM MOVE.

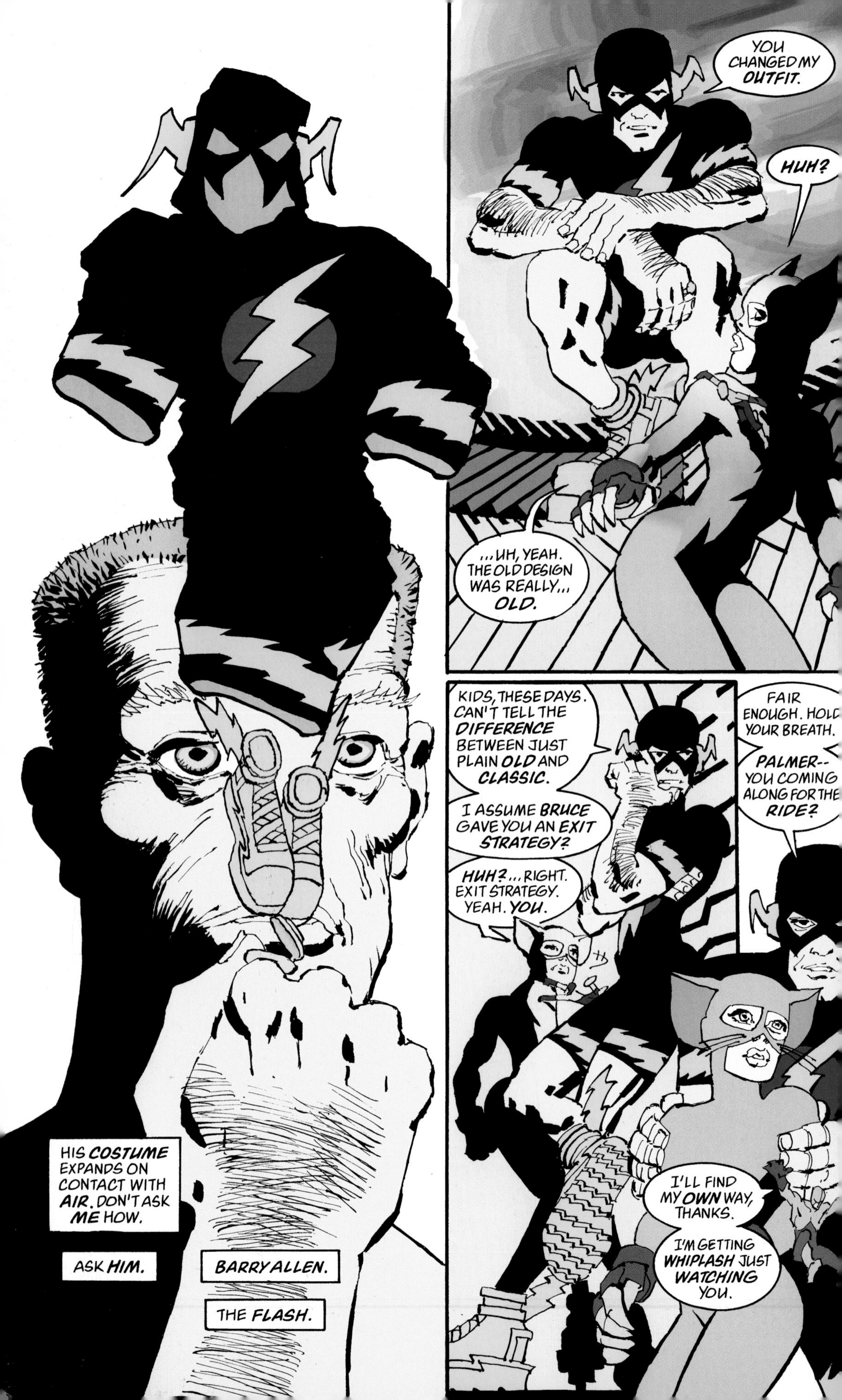

HIS COSTUME EXPANDS ON CONTACT WITH AIR. DON'T ASK ME HOW.
ASK HIM.
BARRY ALLEN.
THE FLASH.
YOU CHANGED MY OUTFIT.
HUH?
...UH, YEAH. THE OLD DESIGN WAS REALLY... OLD.
KIDS, THESE DAYS. CAN'T TELL THE DIFFERENCE BETWEEN JUST PLAIN OLD AND CLASSIC.
I ASSUME BRUCE GAVE YOU AN EXIT STRATEGY?
HUH?... RIGHT. EXIT STRATEGY. YEAH. YOU.
FAIR ENOUGH. HOLD YOUR BREATH.
PALMER-- YOU COMING ALONG FOR THE RIDE?
I'LL FIND MY OWN WAY, THANKS.
I'M GETTING WHIPLASH JUST WATCHING YOU.

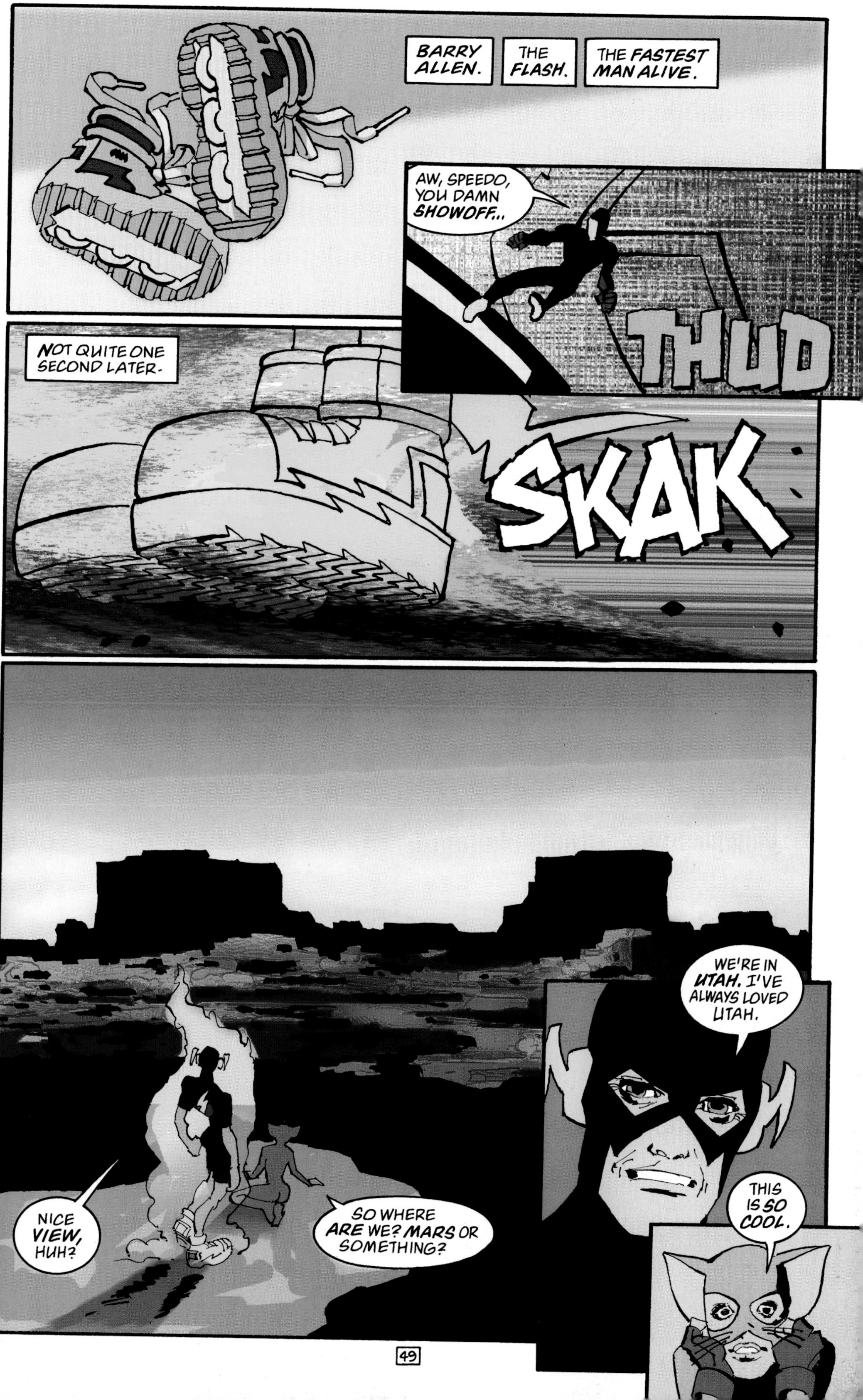
BARRY ALLEN.
THE FLASH.
THE FASTEST MAN ALIVE.
AW, SPEEDO, YOU DAMN SHOWOFF...
THUD
NOT QUITE ONE SECOND LATER-
SKAK
NICE VIEW, HUH?
SO WHERE ARE WE? MARS OR SOMETHING?
WE'RE IN UTAH. I'VE ALWAYS LOVED UTAH.
THIS IS SO COOL.

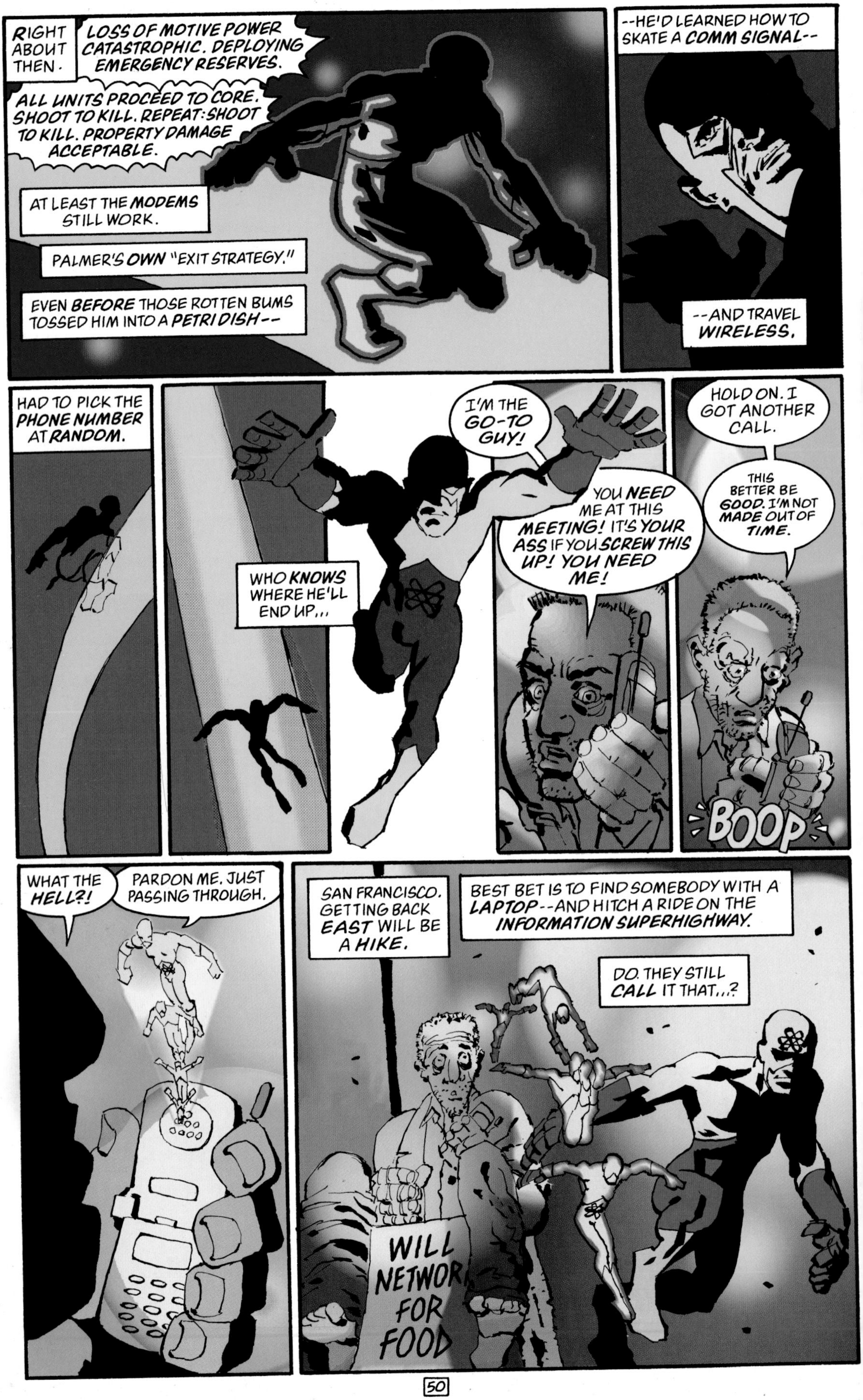
RIGHT ABOUT THEN.
LOSS OF MOTIVE POWER CATASTROPHIC. DEPLOYING EMERGENCY RESERVES.
ALL UNITS PROCEED TO CORE. SHOOT TO KILL. REPEAT: SHOOT TO KILL. PROPERTY DAMAGE ACCEPTABLE.
AT LEAST THE MODEMS STILL WORK.
PALMER'S OWN "EXIT STRATEGY."
EVEN BEFORE THOSE ROTTEN BUMS TOSSED HIM INTO A PETRI DISH--
--HE'D LEARNED HOW TO SKATE A COMM SIGNAL--
--AND TRAVEL WIRELESS.
HAD TO PICK THE PHONE NUMBER AT RANDOM.
WHO KNOWS WHERE HE'LL END UP...
I'M THE GO-TO GUY!
YOU NEED ME AT THIS MEETING! IT'S YOUR ASS IF YOU SCREW THIS UP! YOU NEED ME!
HOLD ON. I GOT ANOTHER CALL.
THIS BETTER BE GOOD. I'M NOT MADE OUT OF TIME.
BOOP
WHAT THE HELL?!
PARDON ME. JUST PASSING THROUGH.
SAN FRANCISCO. GETTING BACK EAST WILL BE A HIKE.
BEST BET IS TO FIND SOMEBODY WITH A LAPTOP--AND HITCH A RIDE ON THE INFORMATION SUPERHIGHWAY.
DO. THEY STILL CALL IT THAT...?
WILL NETWORK FOR FOOD

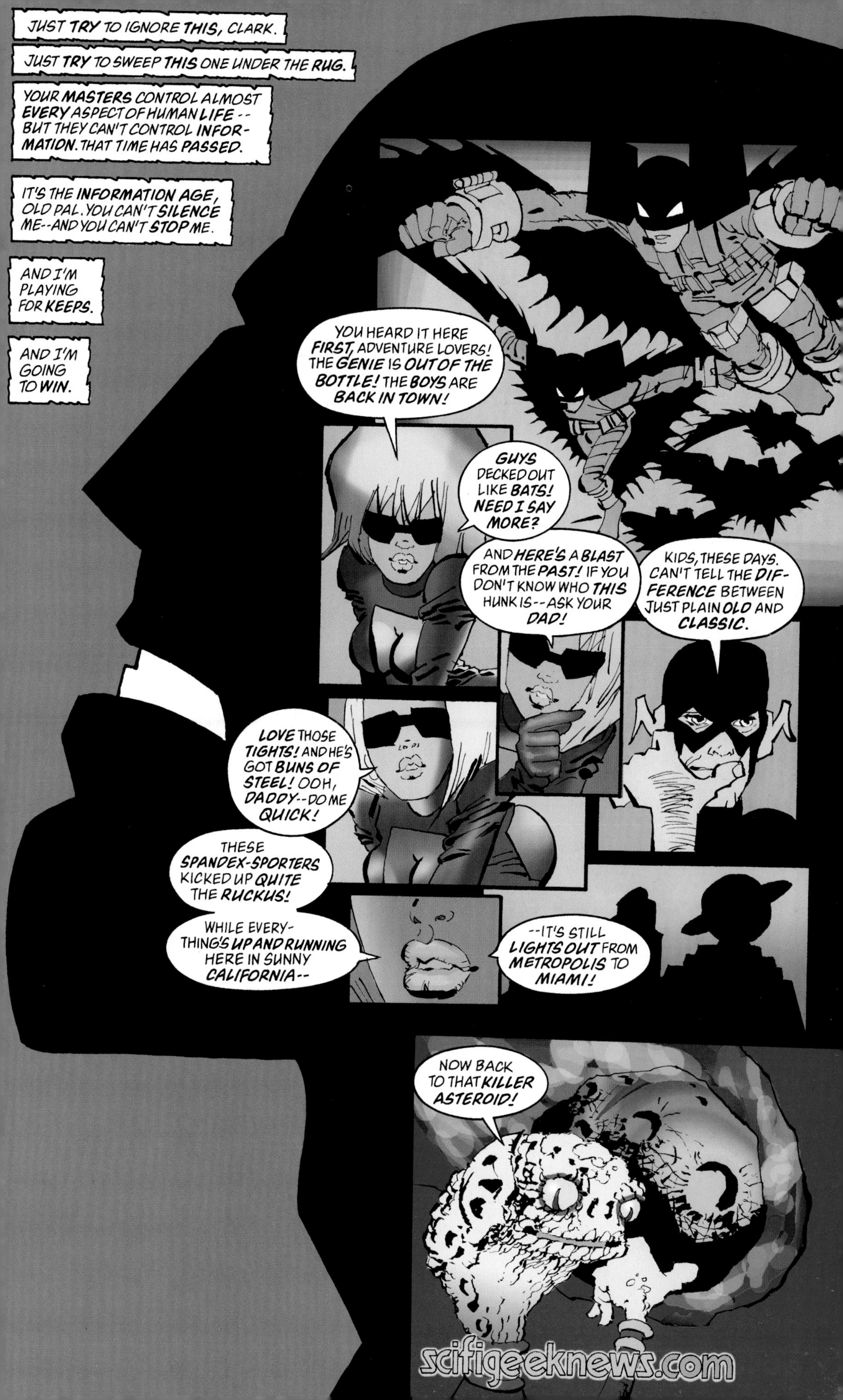
JUST TRY TO IGNORE THIS, CLARK.
JUST TRY TO SWEEP THIS ONE UNDER THE RUG.
YOUR MASTERS CONTROL ALMOST EVERY ASPECT OF HUMAN LIFE -- BUT THEY CAN'T CONTROL INFORMATION. THAT TIME HAS PASSED.
IT'S THE INFORMATION AGE, OLD PAL. YOU CAN'T SILENCE ME--AND YOU CAN'T STOP ME.
AND I'M PLAYING FOR KEEPS.
AND I'M GOING TO WIN.
YOU HEARD IT HERE FIRST, ADVENTURE LOVERS! THE GENIE IS OUT OF THE BOTTLE! THE BOYS ARE BACK IN TOWN!
GUYS DECKED OUT LIKE BATS! NEED I SAY MORE?
AND HERE'S A BLAST FROM THE PAST! IF YOU DON'T KNOW WHO THIS HUNK IS--ASK YOUR DAD!
KIDS, THESE DAYS. CAN'T TELL THE DIFFERENCE BETWEEN JUST PLAIN OLD AND CLASSIC.
LOVE THOSE TIGHTS! AND HE'S GOT BUNS OF STEEL! OOH, DADDY--DO ME QUICK!
THESE SPANDEX-SPORTERS KICKED UP QUITE THE RUCKUS!
WHILE EVERYTHING'S UP AND RUNNING HERE IN SUNNY CALIFORNIA--
--IT'S STILL LIGHTS OUT FROM METROPOLIS TO MIAMI!
NOW BACK TO THAT KILLER ASTEROID!

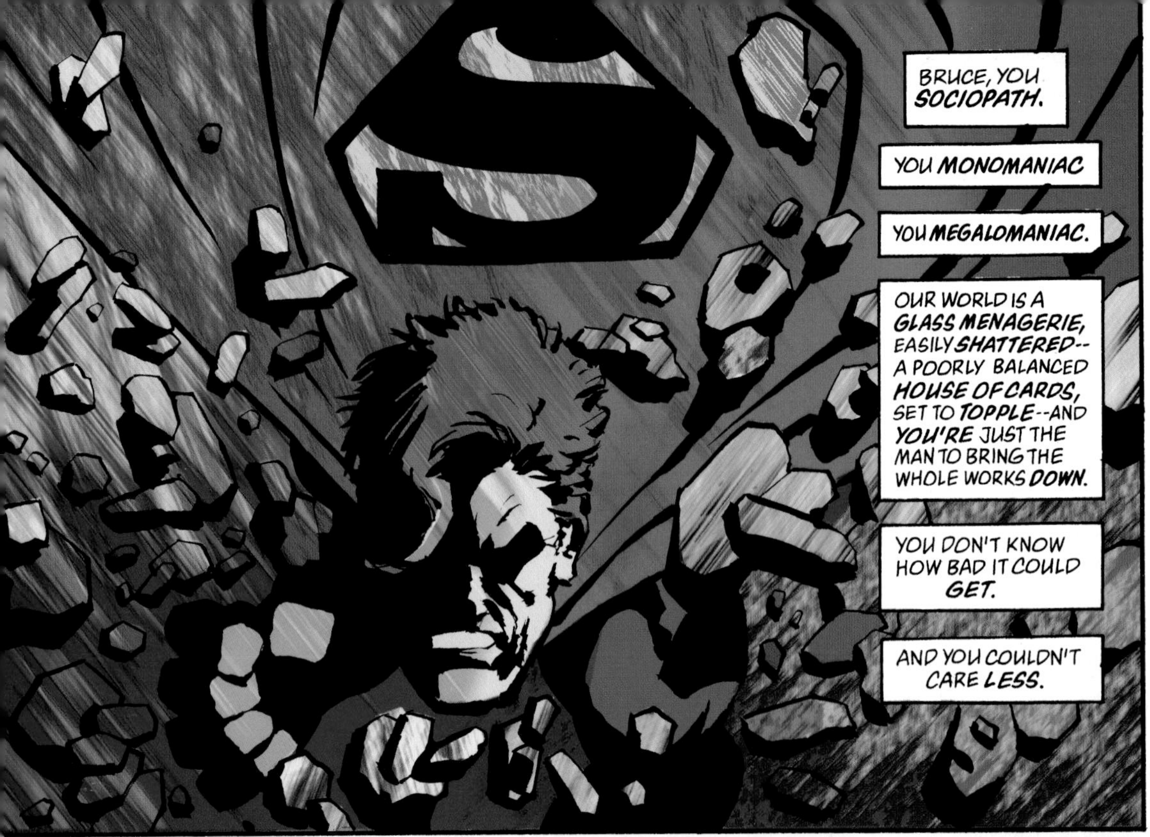
BRUCE, YOU SOCIOPATH.
YOU MONOMANIAC
YOU MEGALOMANIAC.
OUR WORLD IS A GLASS MENAGERIE, EASILY SHATTERED-- A POORLY BALANCED HOUSE OF CARDS, SET TO TOPPLE--AND YOU'RE JUST THE MAN TO BRING THE WHOLE WORKS DOWN.
YOU DON'T KNOW HOW BAD IT COULD GET.
AND YOU COULDN'T CARE LESS.
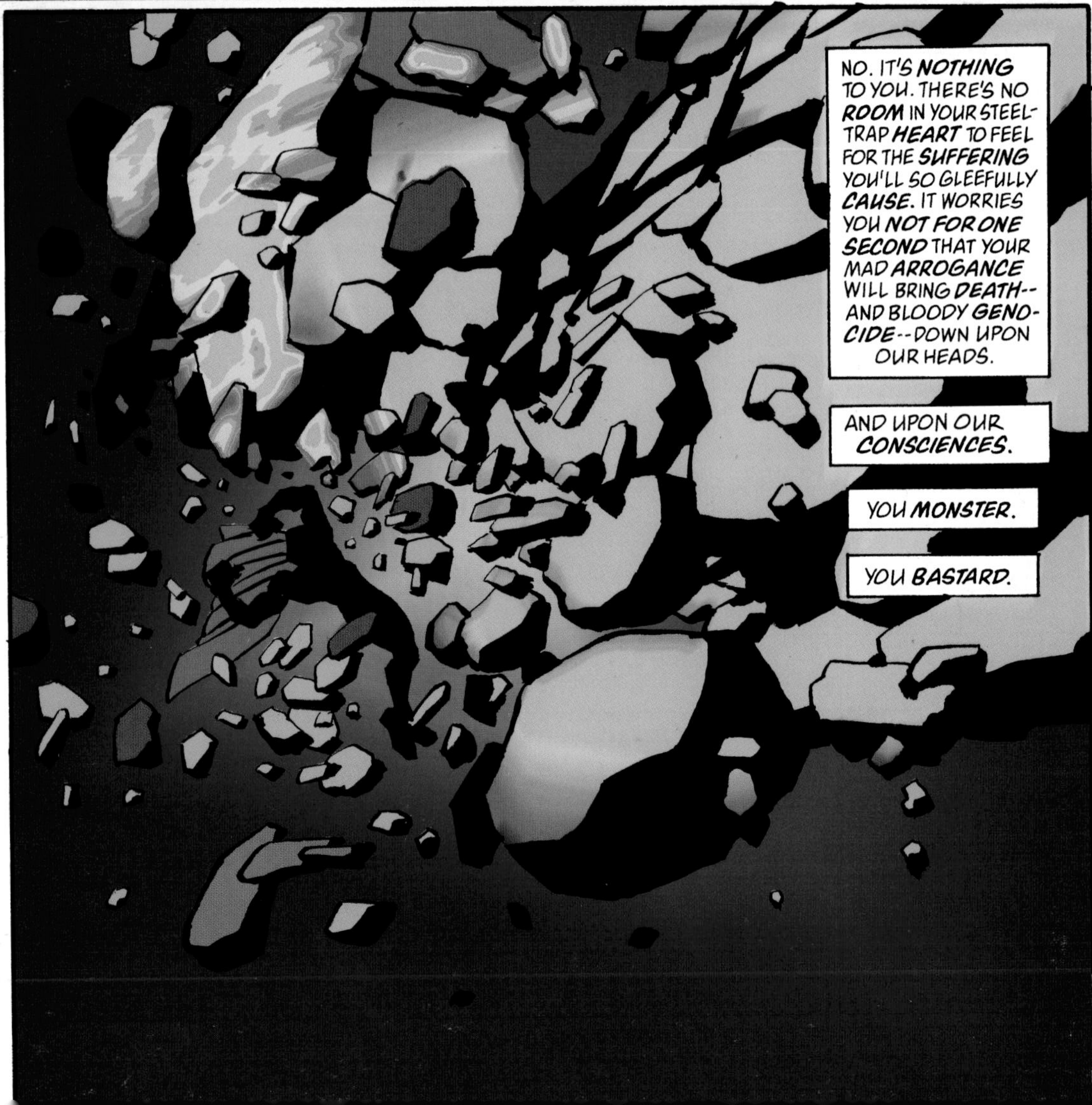
NO. IT'S NOTHING TO YOU. THERE'S NO ROOM IN YOUR STEEL-TRAP HEART TO FEEL FOR THE SUFFERING YOU'LL SO GLEEFULLY CAUSE. IT WORRIES YOU NOT FOR ONE SECOND THAT YOUR MAD ARROGANCE WILL BRING DEATH-- AND BLOODY GENOCIDE--DOWN UPON OUR HEADS.
AND UPON OUR CONSCIENCES.
YOU MONSTER.
YOU BASTARD.

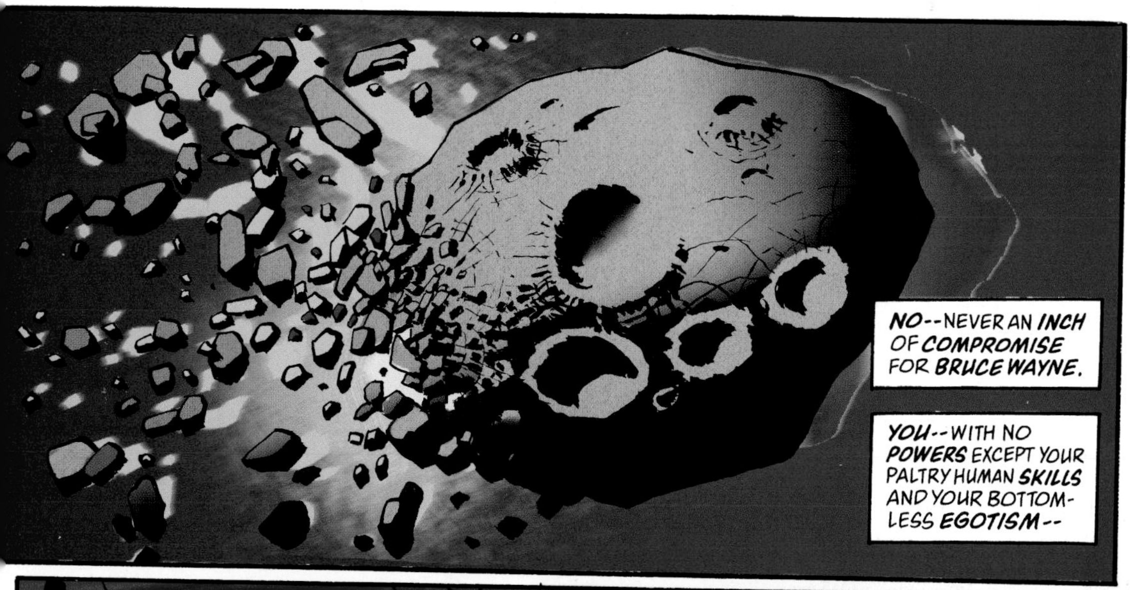
NO--NEVER AN INCH OF COMPROMISE FOR BRUCE WAYNE.
YOU--WITH NO POWERS EXCEPT YOUR PALTRY HUMAN SKILLS AND YOUR BOTTOMLESS EGOTISM--

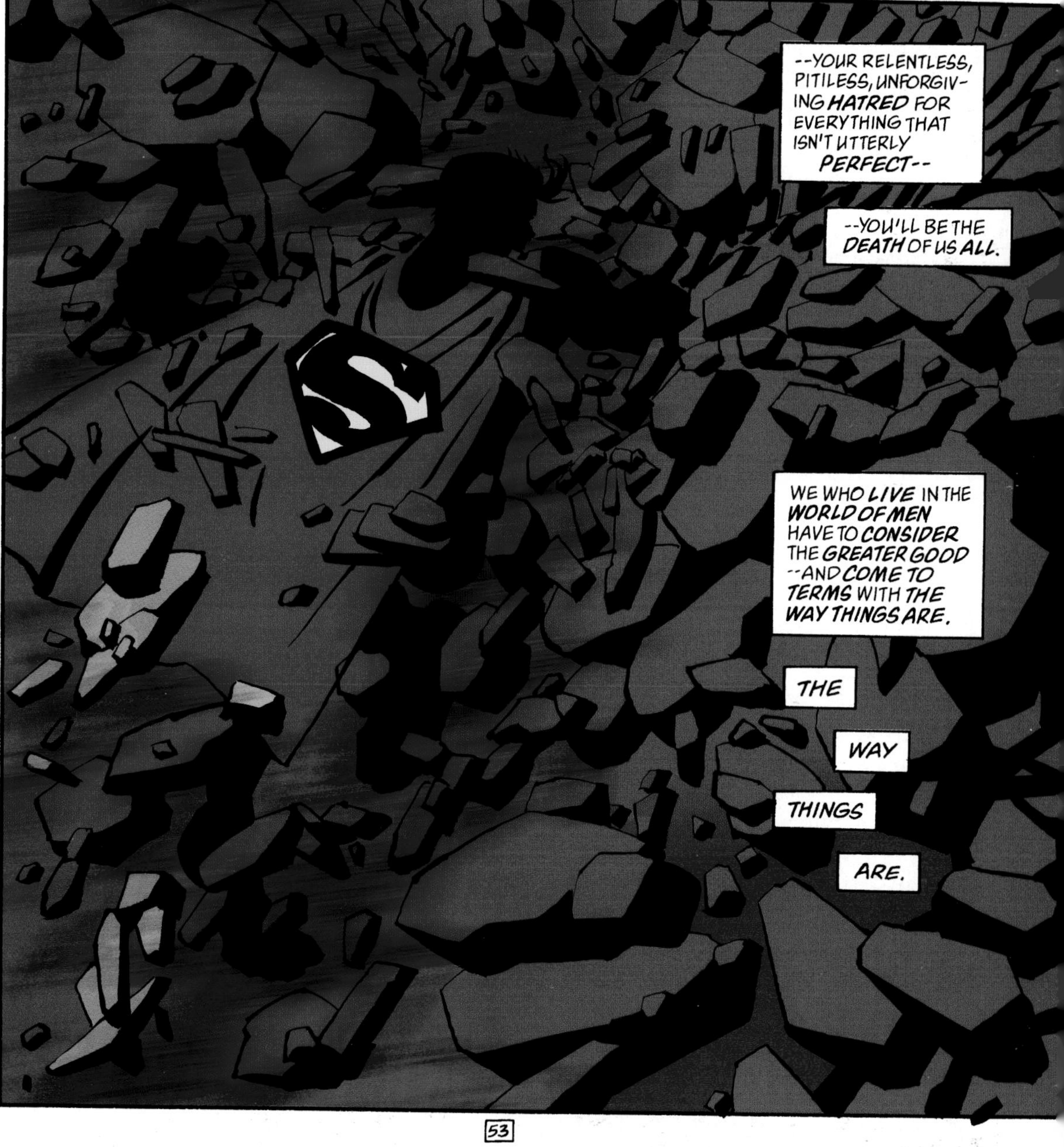
--YOUR RELENTLESS, PITILESS, UNFORGIVING HATRED FOR EVERYTHING THAT ISN'T UTTERLY PERFECT--
--YOU'LL BE THE DEATH OF US ALL.
WE WHO LIVE IN THE WORLD OF MEN HAVE TO CONSIDER THE GREATER GOOD --AND COME TO TERMS WITH THE WAY THINGS ARE.
THE
WAY
THINGS
ARE.

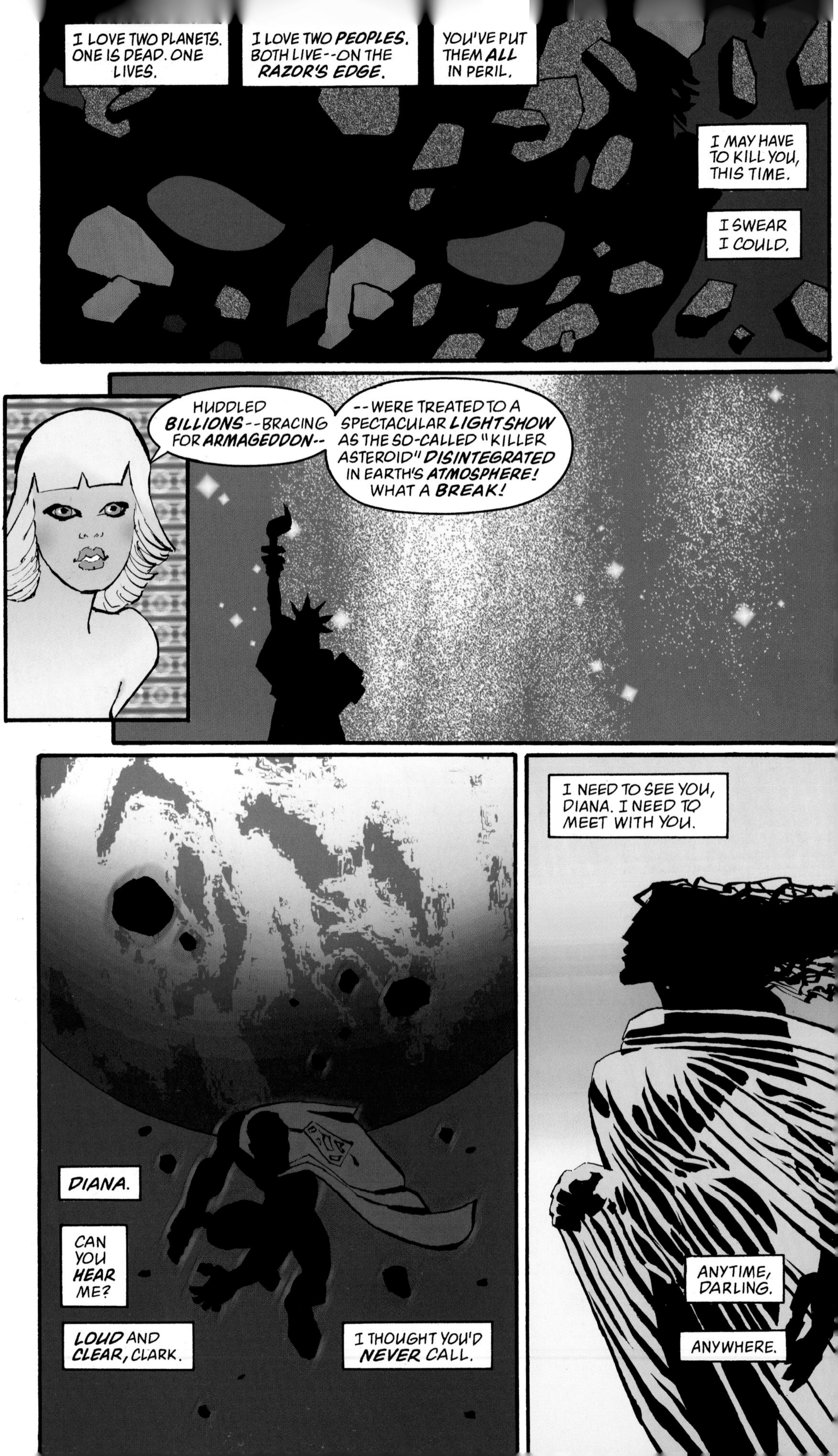

I LOVE TWO PLANETS. ONE IS DEAD. ONE LIVES.
I LOVE TWO PEOPLES. BOTH LIVE--ON THE RAZOR'S EDGE.
YOU'VE PUT THEM ALL IN PERIL.
I MAY HAVE TO KILL YOU, THIS TIME.
I SWEAR I COULD.
HUDDLED BILLIONS--BRACING FOR ARMAGEDDON--
--WERE TREATED TO A SPECTACULAR LIGHT SHOW AS THE SO-CALLED "KILLER ASTEROID" DISINTEGRATED IN EARTH'S ATMOSPHERE! WHAT A BREAK!
DIANA.
CAN YOU HEAR ME?
LOUD AND CLEAR, CLARK.
I THOUGHT YOU'D NEVER CALL.
I NEED TO SEE YOU, DIANA. I NEED TO MEET WITH YOU.
ANYTIME, DARLING.
ANYWHERE.

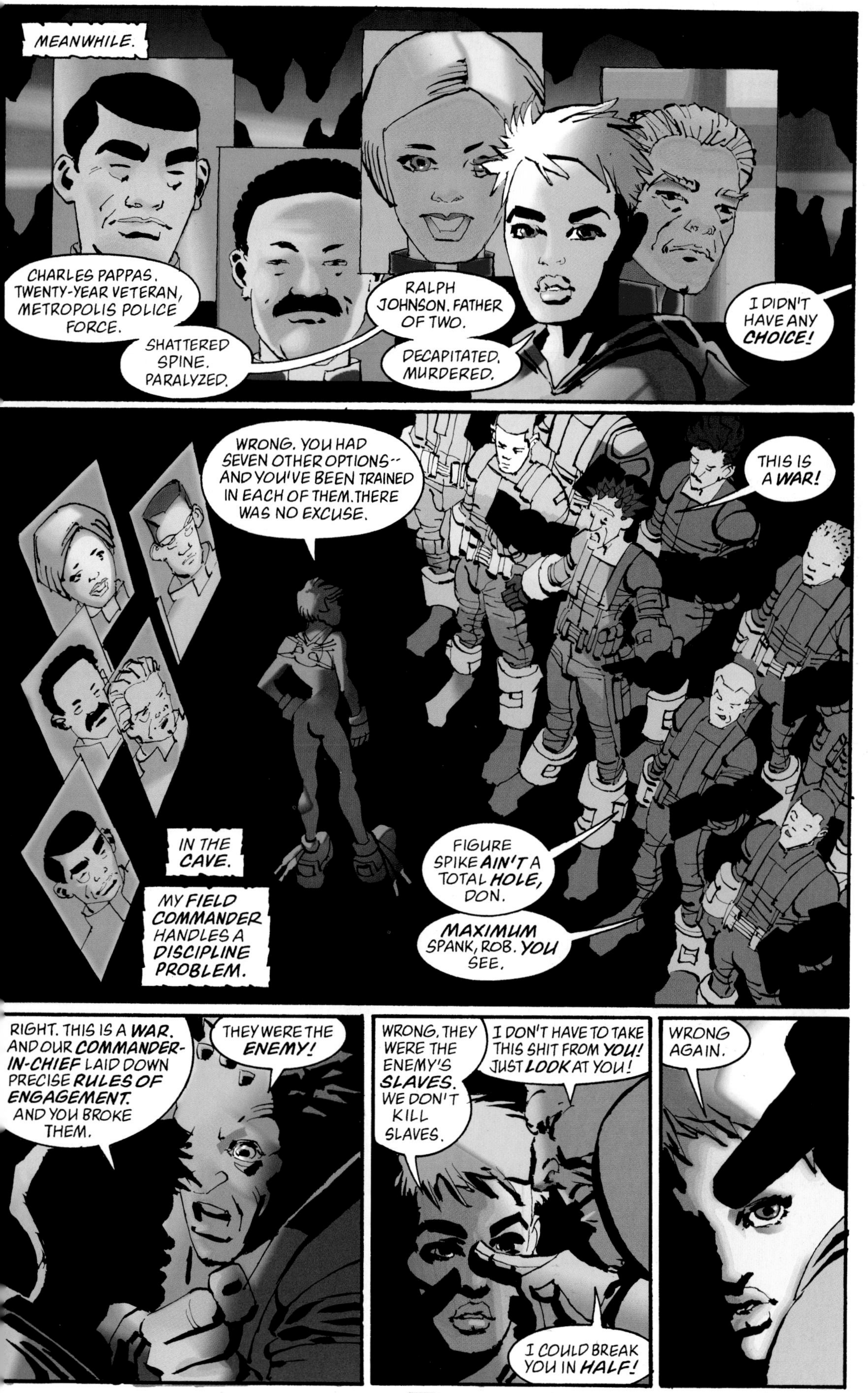
MEANWHILE.
CHARLES PAPPAS. TWENTY-YEAR VETERAN, METROPOLIS POLICE FORCE.
SHATTERED SPINE. PARALYZED.
RALPH JOHNSON. FATHER OF TWO.
DECAPITATED. MURDERED.
I DIDN'T HAVE ANY CHOICE!
WRONG. YOU HAD SEVEN OTHER OPTIONS-- AND YOU'VE BEEN TRAINED IN EACH OF THEM. THERE WAS NO EXCUSE.
THIS IS A WAR!
IN THE CAVE.
MY FIELD COMMANDER HANDLES A DISCIPLINE PROBLEM.
FIGURE SPIKE AIN'T A TOTAL HOLE, DON.
MAXIMUM SPANK, ROB. YOU SEE.
RIGHT. THIS IS A WAR. AND OUR COMMANDER-IN-CHIEF LAID DOWN PRECISE RULES OF ENGAGEMENT. AND YOU BROKE THEM.
THEY WERE THE ENEMY!
WRONG. THEY WERE THE ENEMY'S SLAVES. WE DON'T KILL SLAVES.
I DON'T HAVE TO TAKE THIS SHIT FROM YOU! JUST LOOK AT YOU!
I COULD BREAK YOU IN HALF!
WRONG AGAIN.

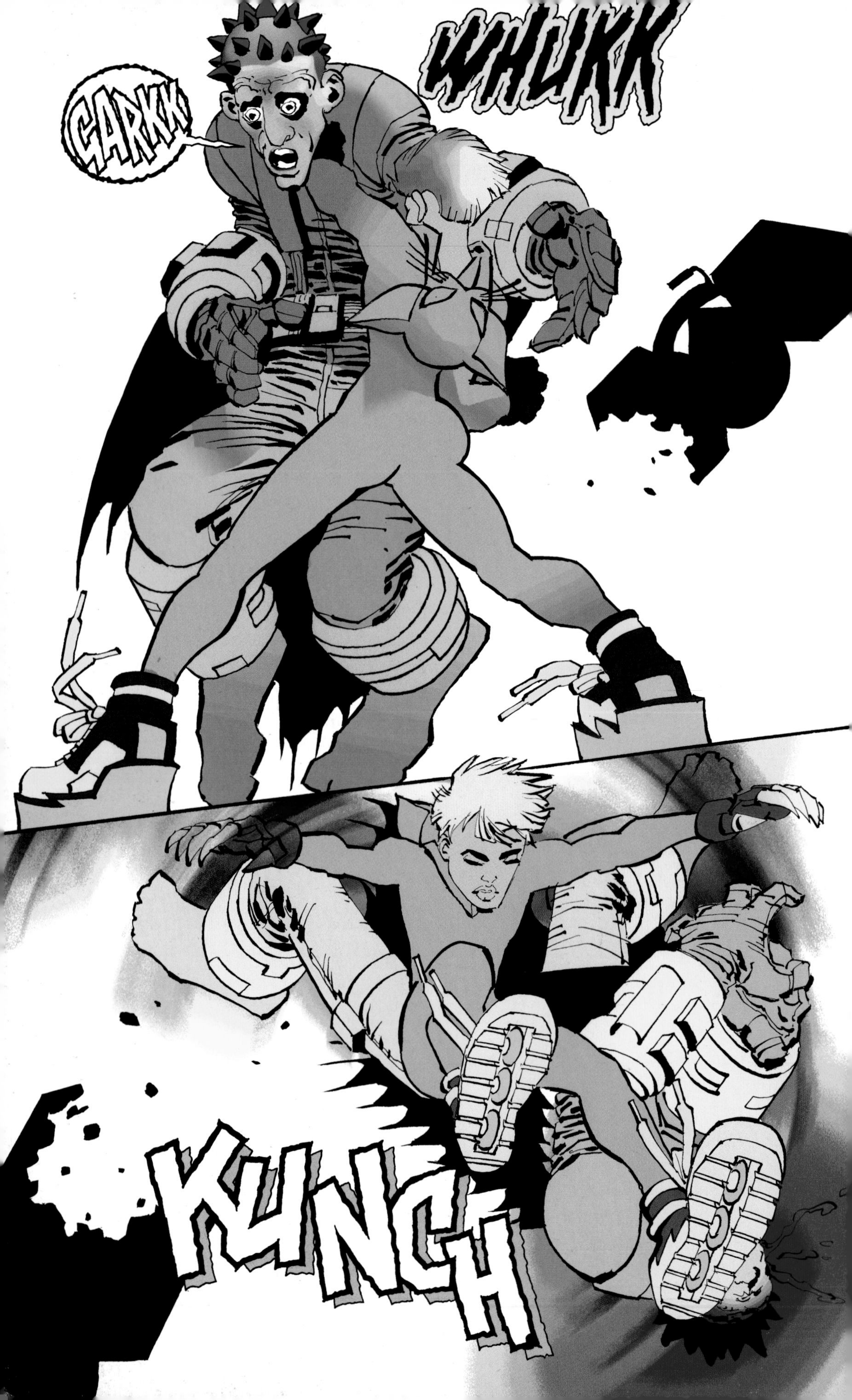
GARKK
WHUKK
KLUNCH

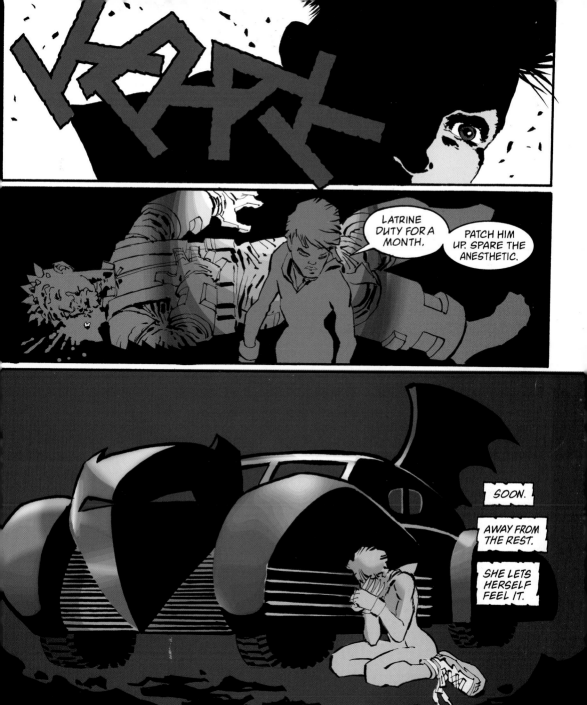

KRRK

LATRINE DUTY FOR A MONTH.

PATCH HIM UP. SPARE THE ANESTHETIC.

SOON.

AWAY FROM THE REST.

SHE LETS HERSELF FEEL IT.

GOOD GIRL. GOOD SOLDIER.

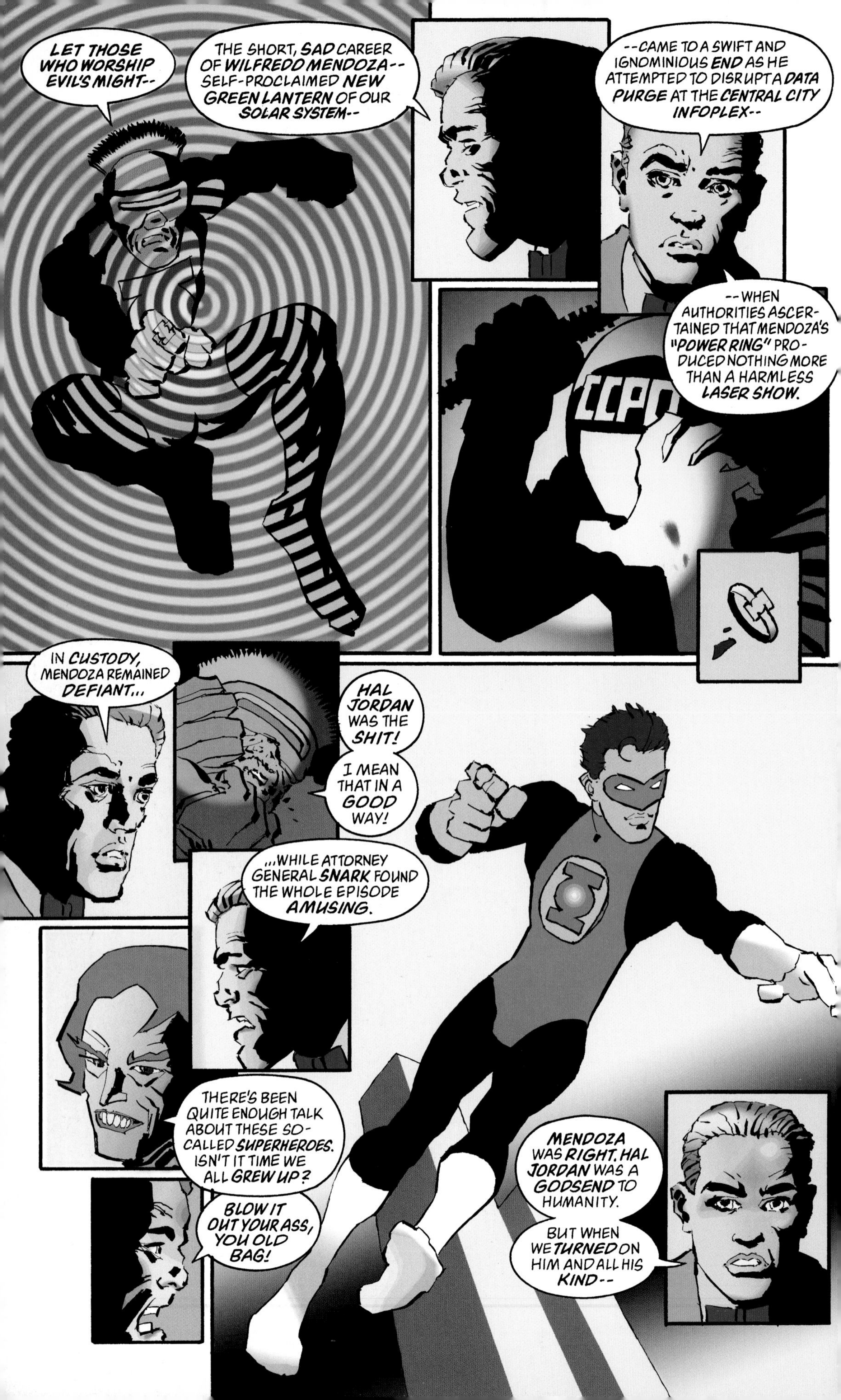
LET THOSE WHO WORSHIP EVIL'S MIGHT--
THE SHORT, SAD CAREER OF WILFREDO MENDOZA-- SELF-PROCLAIMED NEW GREEN LANTERN OF OUR SOLAR SYSTEM--
--CAME TO A SWIFT AND IGNOMINIOUS END AS HE ATTEMPTED TO DISRUPT A DATA PURGE AT THE CENTRAL CITY INFOPLEX--
--WHEN AUTHORITIES ASCERTAINED THAT MENDOZA'S "POWER RING" PRODUCED NOTHING MORE THAN A HARMLESS LASER SHOW.
CCPD
IN CUSTODY, MENDOZA REMAINED DEFIANT...
HAL JORDAN WAS THE SHIT!
I MEAN THAT IN A GOOD WAY!
...WHILE ATTORNEY GENERAL SNARK FOUND THE WHOLE EPISODE AMUSING.
THERE'S BEEN QUITE ENOUGH TALK ABOUT THESE SO-CALLED SUPERHEROES. ISN'T IT TIME WE ALL GREW UP?
BLOW IT OUT YOUR ASS, YOU OLD BAG!
MENDOZA WAS RIGHT. HAL JORDAN WAS A GODSEND TO HUMANITY.
BUT WHEN WE TURNED ON HIM AND ALL HIS KIND--

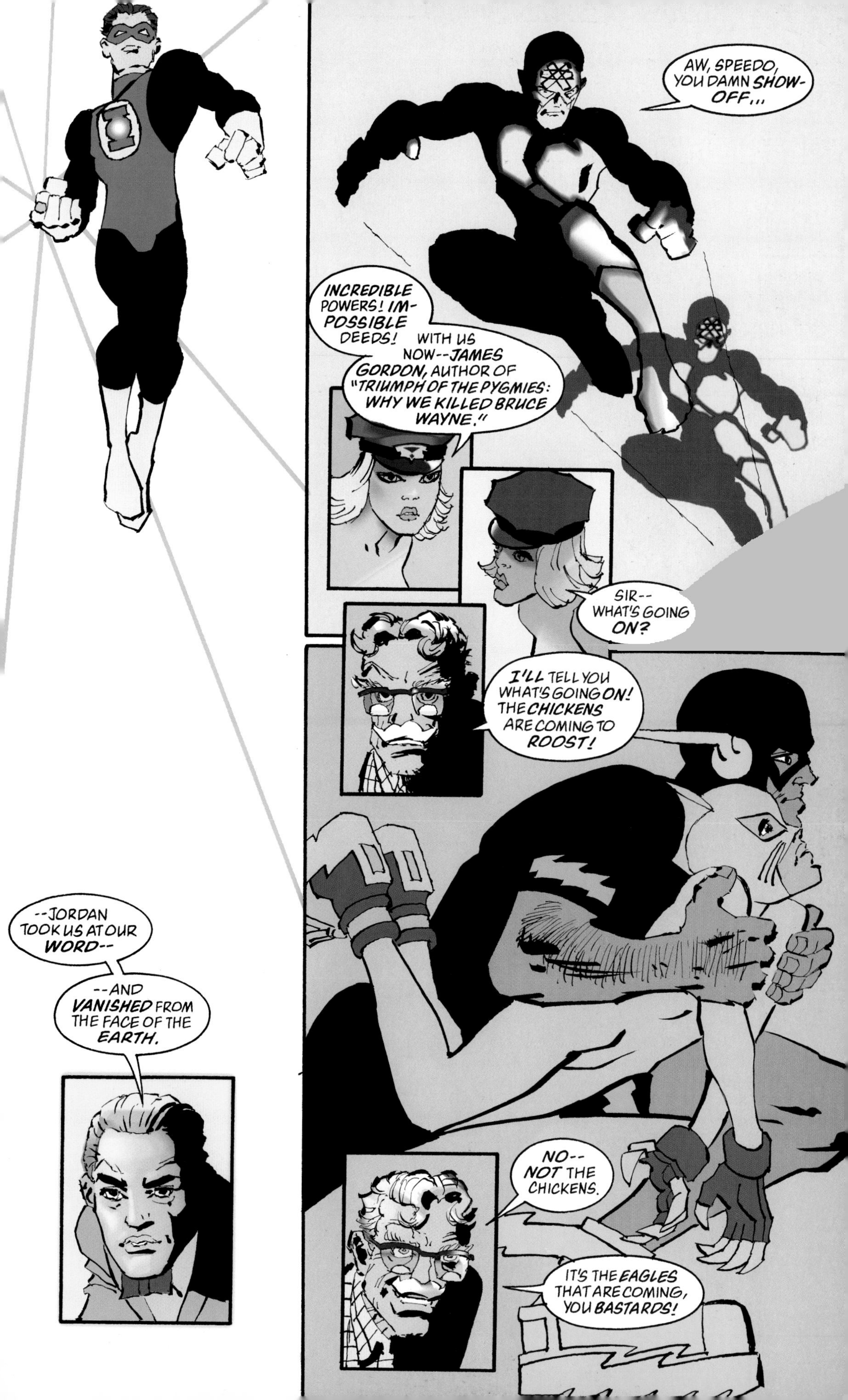
AW, SPEEDO, YOU DAMN SHOW-OFF...
INCREDIBLE POWERS! IMPOSSIBLE DEEDS!
WITH US NOW--JAMES GORDON, AUTHOR OF "TRIUMPH OF THE PYGMIES: WHY WE KILLED BRUCE WAYNE."
SIR--WHAT'S GOING ON?
I'LL TELL YOU WHAT'S GOING ON! THE CHICKENS ARE COMING TO ROOST!
--JORDAN TOOK US AT OUR WORD--
--AND VANISHED FROM THE FACE OF THE EARTH.
NO--NOT THE CHICKENS.
IT'S THE EAGLES THAT ARE COMING, YOU BASTARDS!

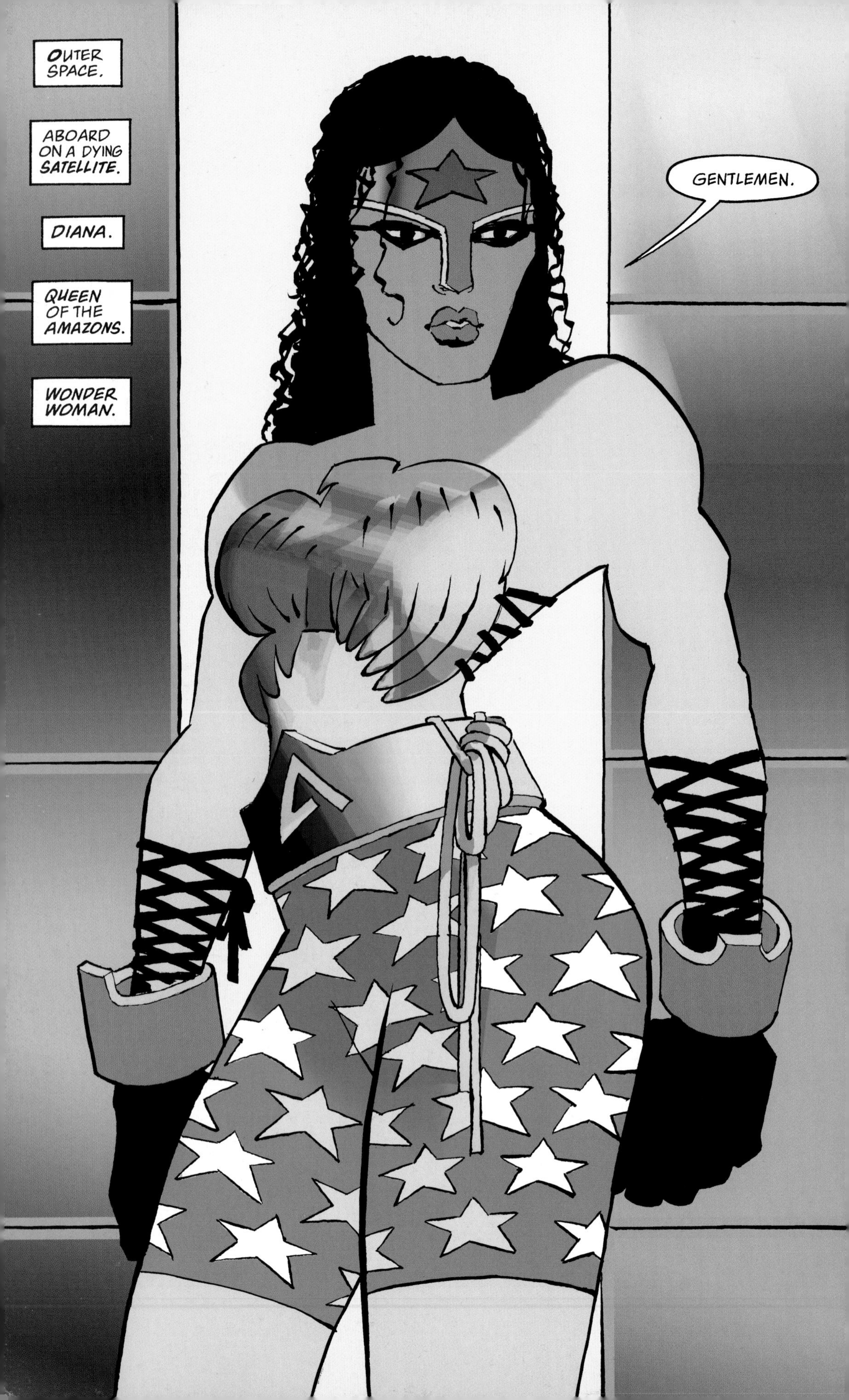
OUTER SPACE.
ABOARD ON A DYING SATELLITE.
DIANA.
QUEEN OF THE AMAZONS.
WONDER WOMAN.
GENTLEMEN.

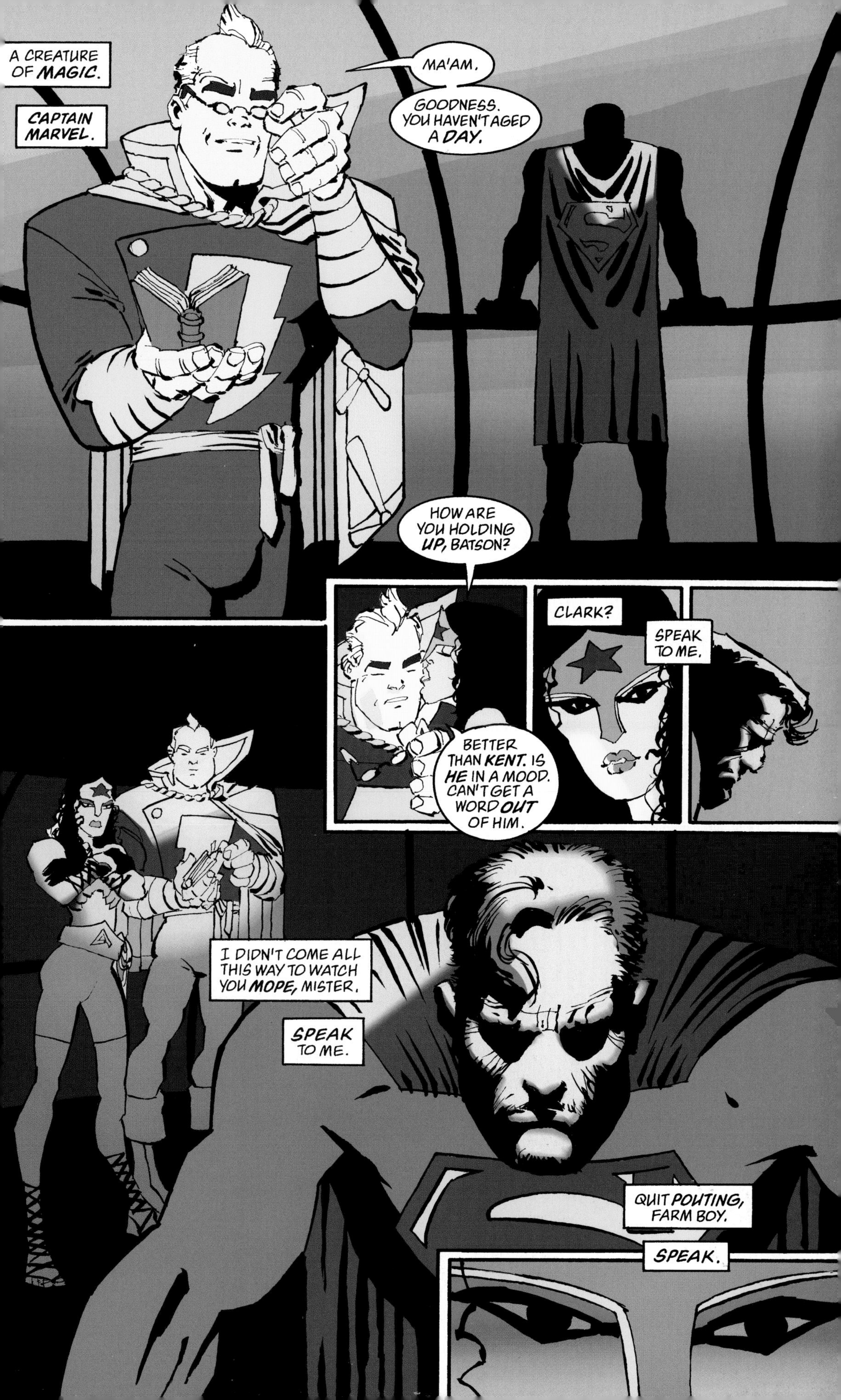
A CREATURE OF MAGIC.
CAPTAIN MARVEL.
MA'AM.
GOODNESS. YOU HAVEN'T AGED A DAY.
HOW ARE YOU HOLDING UP, BATSON?
BETTER THAN KENT. IS HE IN A MOOD. CAN'T GET A WORD OUT OF HIM.
CLARK?
SPEAK TO ME.
I DIDN'T COME ALL THIS WAY TO WATCH YOU MOPE, MISTER.
SPEAK TO ME.
QUIT POUTING, FARM BOY.
SPEAK.

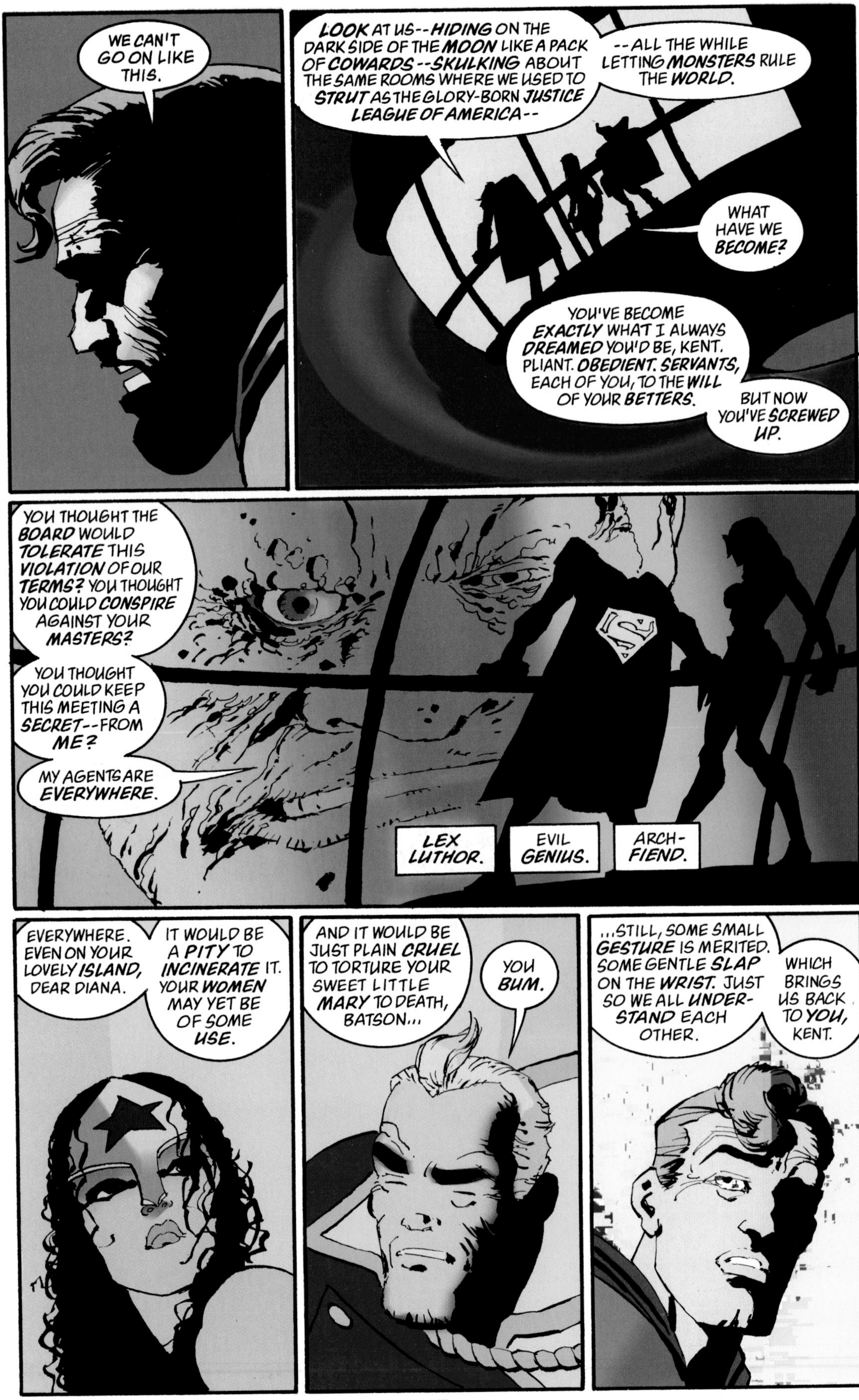
WE CAN'T GO ON LIKE THIS.
LOOK AT US--HIDING ON THE DARK SIDE OF THE MOON LIKE A PACK OF COWARDS--SKULKING ABOUT THE SAME ROOMS WHERE WE USED TO STRUT AS THE GLORY-BORN JUSTICE LEAGUE OF AMERICA--
--ALL THE WHILE LETTING MONSTERS RULE THE WORLD.
WHAT HAVE WE BECOME?
YOU'VE BECOME EXACTLY WHAT I ALWAYS DREAMED YOU'D BE, KENT. PLIANT. OBEDIENT. SERVANTS, EACH OF YOU, TO THE WILL OF YOUR BETTERS.
BUT NOW YOU'VE SCREWED UP.
YOU THOUGHT THE BOARD WOULD TOLERATE THIS VIOLATION OF OUR TERMS? YOU THOUGHT YOU COULD CONSPIRE AGAINST YOUR MASTERS?
YOU THOUGHT YOU COULD KEEP THIS MEETING A SECRET--FROM ME?
MY AGENTS ARE EVERYWHERE.
LEX LUTHOR.
EVIL GENIUS.
ARCH-FIEND.
EVERYWHERE. EVEN ON YOUR LOVELY ISLAND, DEAR DIANA.
IT WOULD BE A PITY TO INCINERATE IT. YOUR WOMEN MAY YET BE OF SOME USE.
AND IT WOULD BE JUST PLAIN CRUEL TO TORTURE YOUR SWEET LITTLE MARY TO DEATH, BATSON...
YOU BUM.
...STILL, SOME SMALL GESTURE IS MERITED. SOME GENTLE SLAP ON THE WRIST. JUST SO WE ALL UNDERSTAND EACH OTHER.
WHICH BRINGS US BACK TO YOU, KENT.

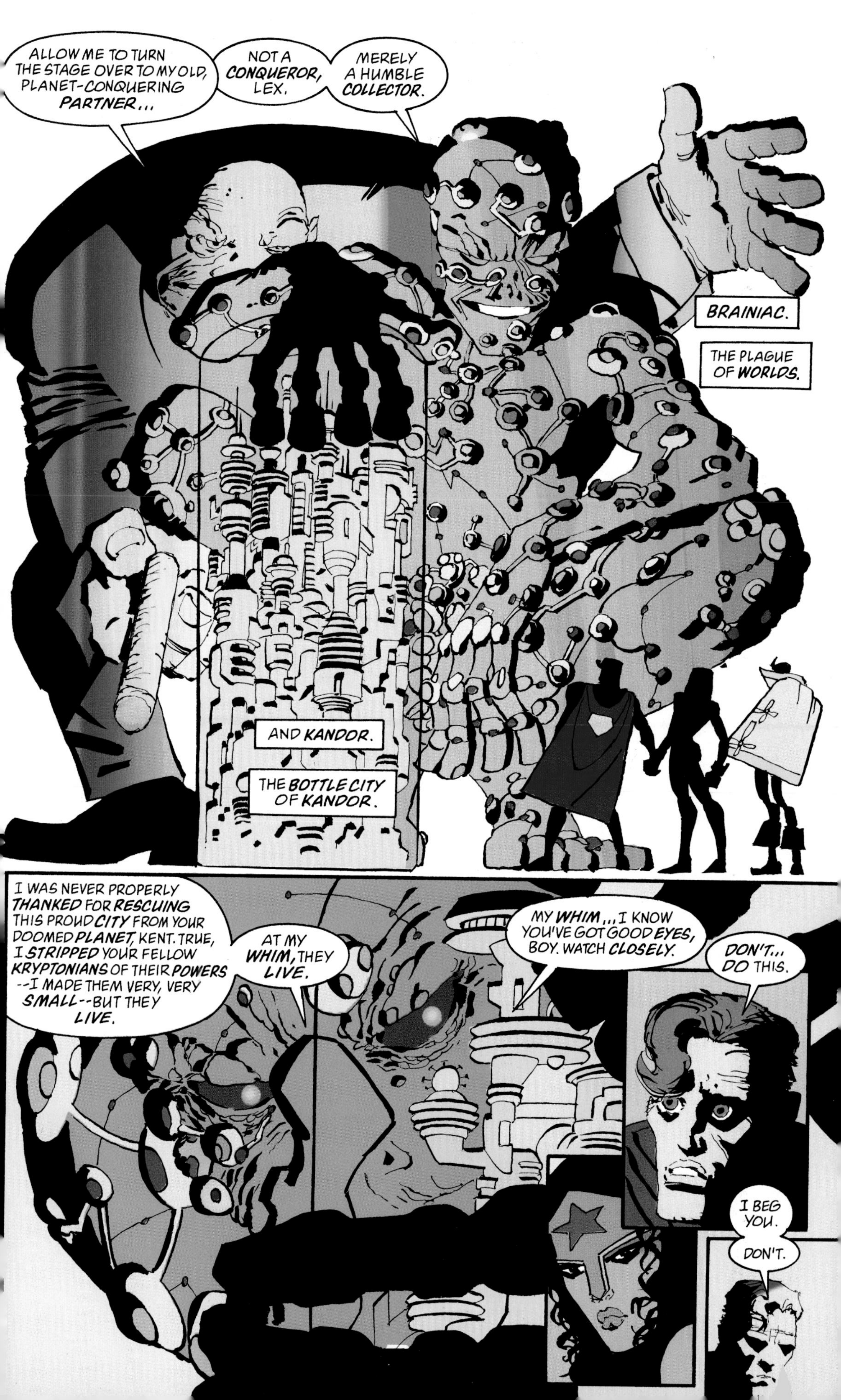
ALLOW ME TO TURN THE STAGE OVER TO MY OLD, PLANET-CONQUERING PARTNER...
NOT A CONQUEROR, LEX.
MERELY A HUMBLE COLLECTOR.
BRAINIAC.
THE PLAGUE OF WORLDS.
AND KANDOR.
THE BOTTLE CITY OF KANDOR.
I WAS NEVER PROPERLY THANKED FOR RESCUING THIS PROUD CITY FROM YOUR DOOMED PLANET, KENT. TRUE, I STRIPPED YOUR FELLOW KRYPTONIANS OF THEIR POWERS --I MADE THEM VERY, VERY SMALL--BUT THEY LIVE.
AT MY WHIM, THEY LIVE.
MY WHIM... I KNOW YOU'VE GOT GOOD EYES, BOY. WATCH CLOSELY.
DON'T... DO THIS.
I BEG YOU.
DON'T.

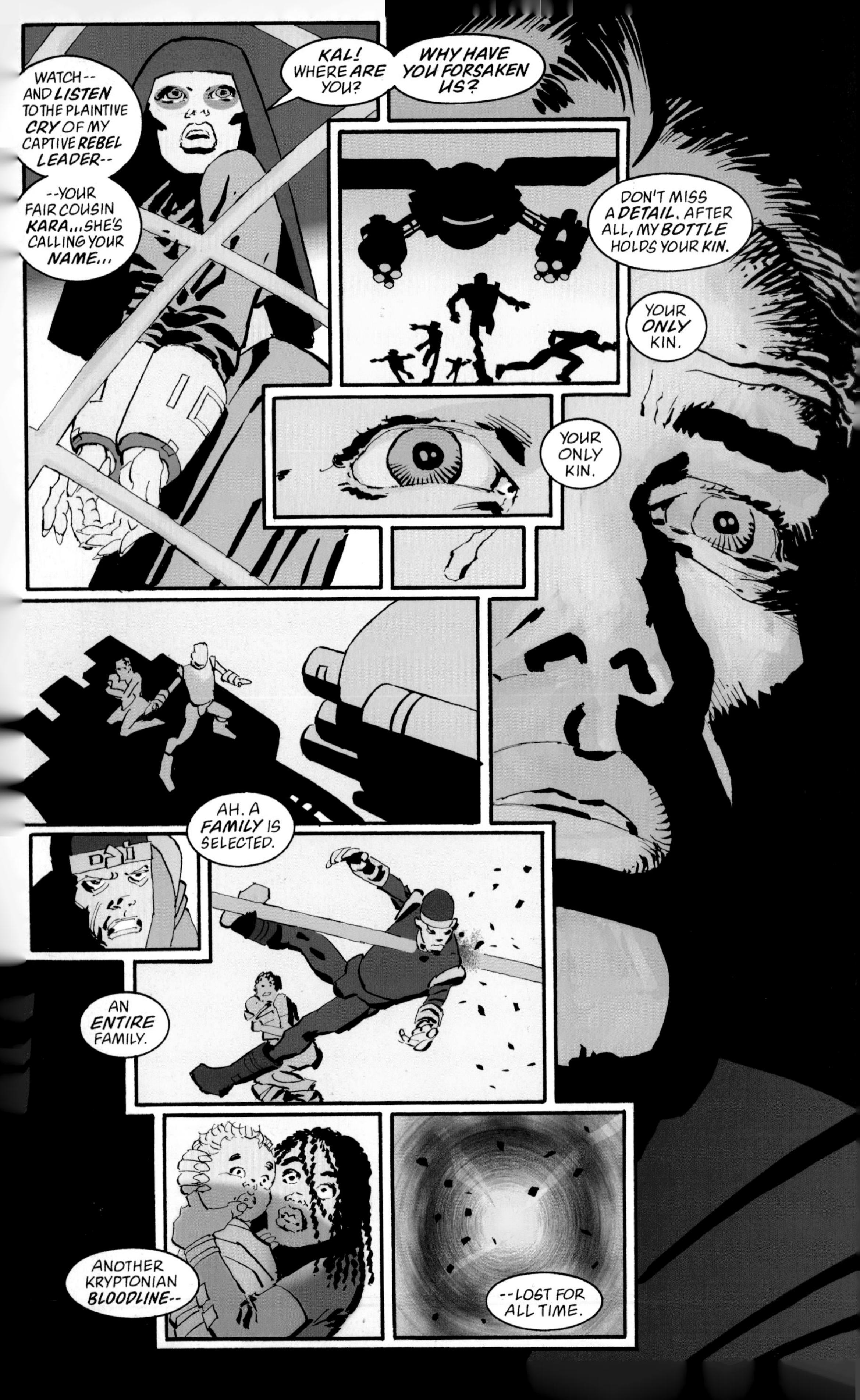

WATCH-- AND LISTEN TO THE PLAINTIVE CRY OF MY CAPTIVE REBEL LEADER--
--YOUR FAIR COUSIN KARA... SHE'S CALLING YOUR NAME...
KAL! WHERE ARE YOU?
WHY HAVE YOU FORSAKEN US?
DON'T MISS A DETAIL. AFTER ALL, MY BOTTLE HOLDS YOUR KIN.
YOUR ONLY KIN.
YOUR ONLY KIN.
AH. A FAMILY IS SELECTED.
AN ENTIRE FAMILY.
ANOTHER KRYPTONIAN BLOODLINE--
--LOST FOR ALL TIME.

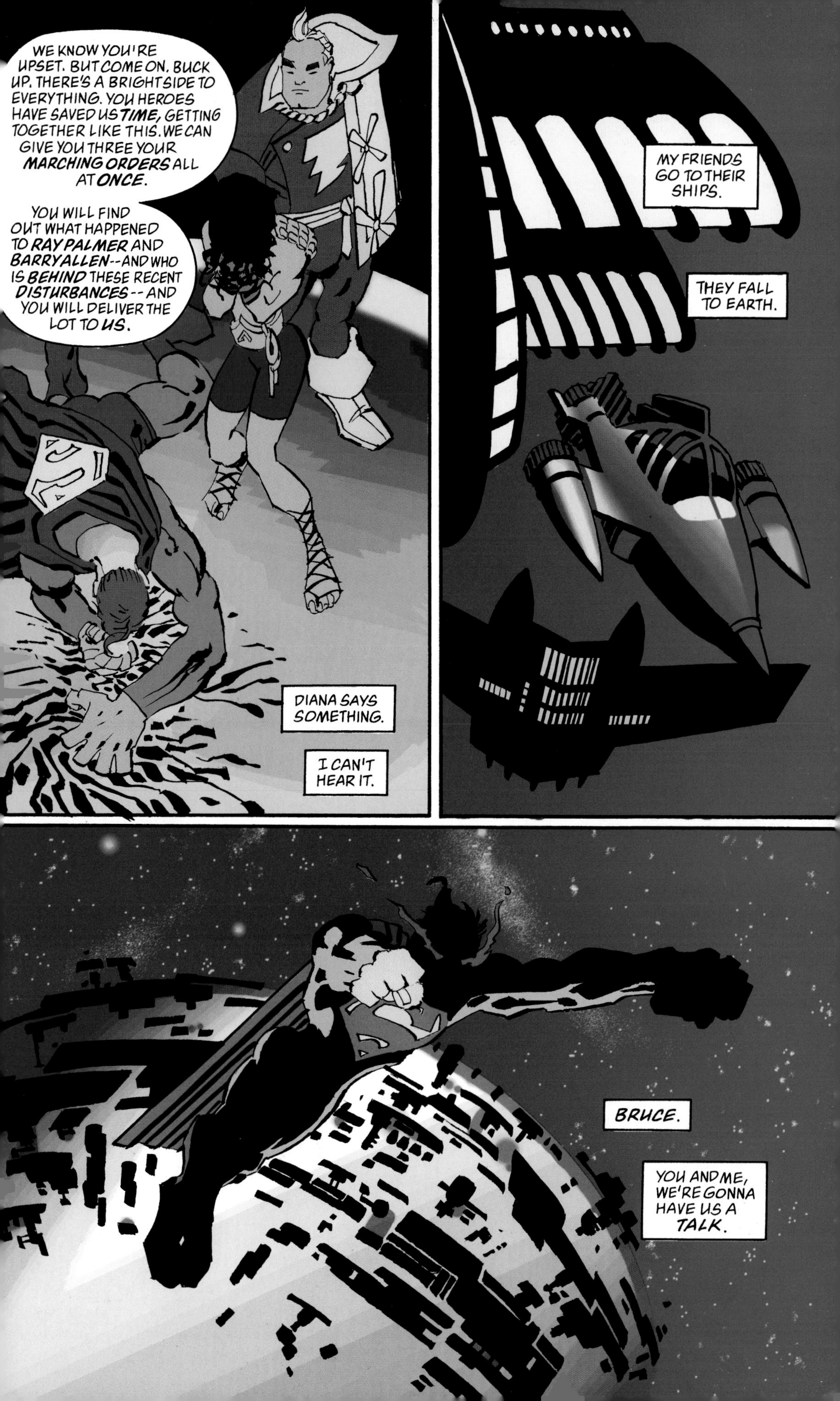

WE KNOW YOU'RE UPSET. BUT COME ON. BUCK UP. THERE'S A BRIGHT SIDE TO EVERYTHING. YOU HEROES HAVE SAVED US TIME, GETTING TOGETHER LIKE THIS. WE CAN GIVE YOU THREE YOUR MARCHING ORDERS ALL AT ONCE.
YOU WILL FIND OUT WHAT HAPPENED TO RAY PALMER AND BARRY ALLEN--AND WHO IS BEHIND THESE RECENT DISTURBANCES--AND YOU WILL DELIVER THE LOT TO US.
DIANA SAYS SOMETHING.
I CAN'T HEAR IT.
MY FRIENDS GO TO THEIR SHIPS.
THEY FALL TO EARTH.
BRUCE.
YOU AND ME, WE'RE GONNA HAVE US A TALK.

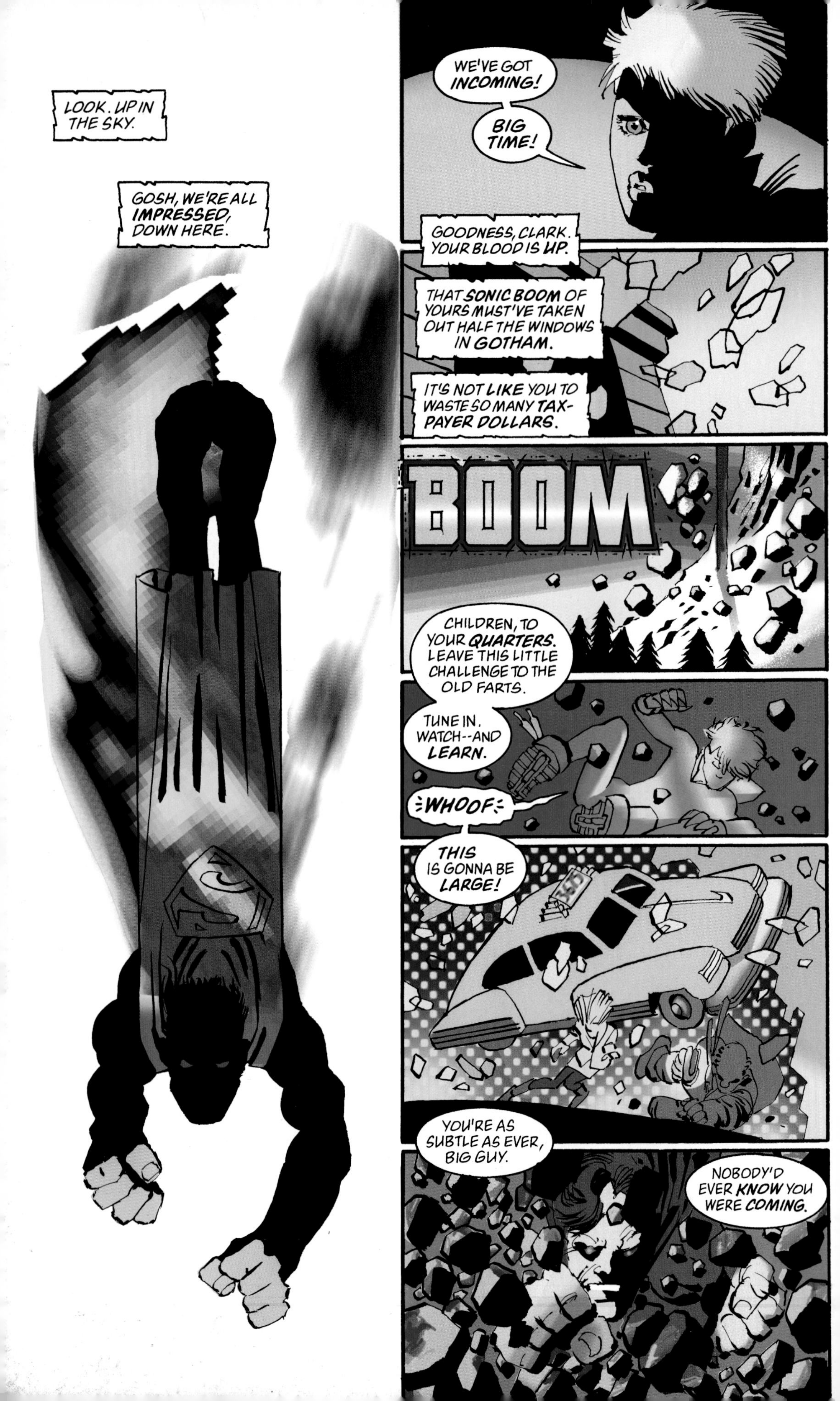
LOOK. UP IN THE SKY.
GOSH, WE'RE ALL IMPRESSED, DOWN HERE.
WE'VE GOT INCOMING!
BIG TIME!
GOODNESS, CLARK. YOUR BLOOD IS UP.
THAT SONIC BOOM OF YOURS MUST'VE TAKEN OUT HALF THE WINDOWS IN GOTHAM.
IT'S NOT LIKE YOU TO WASTE SO MANY TAX-PAYER DOLLARS.
BOOM
CHILDREN, TO YOUR QUARTERS. LEAVE THIS LITTLE CHALLENGE TO THE OLD FARTS.
TUNE IN. WATCH--AND LEARN.
WHOOF
THIS IS GONNA BE LARGE!
YOU'RE AS SUBTLE AS EVER, BIG GUY.
NOBODY'D EVER KNOW YOU WERE COMING.

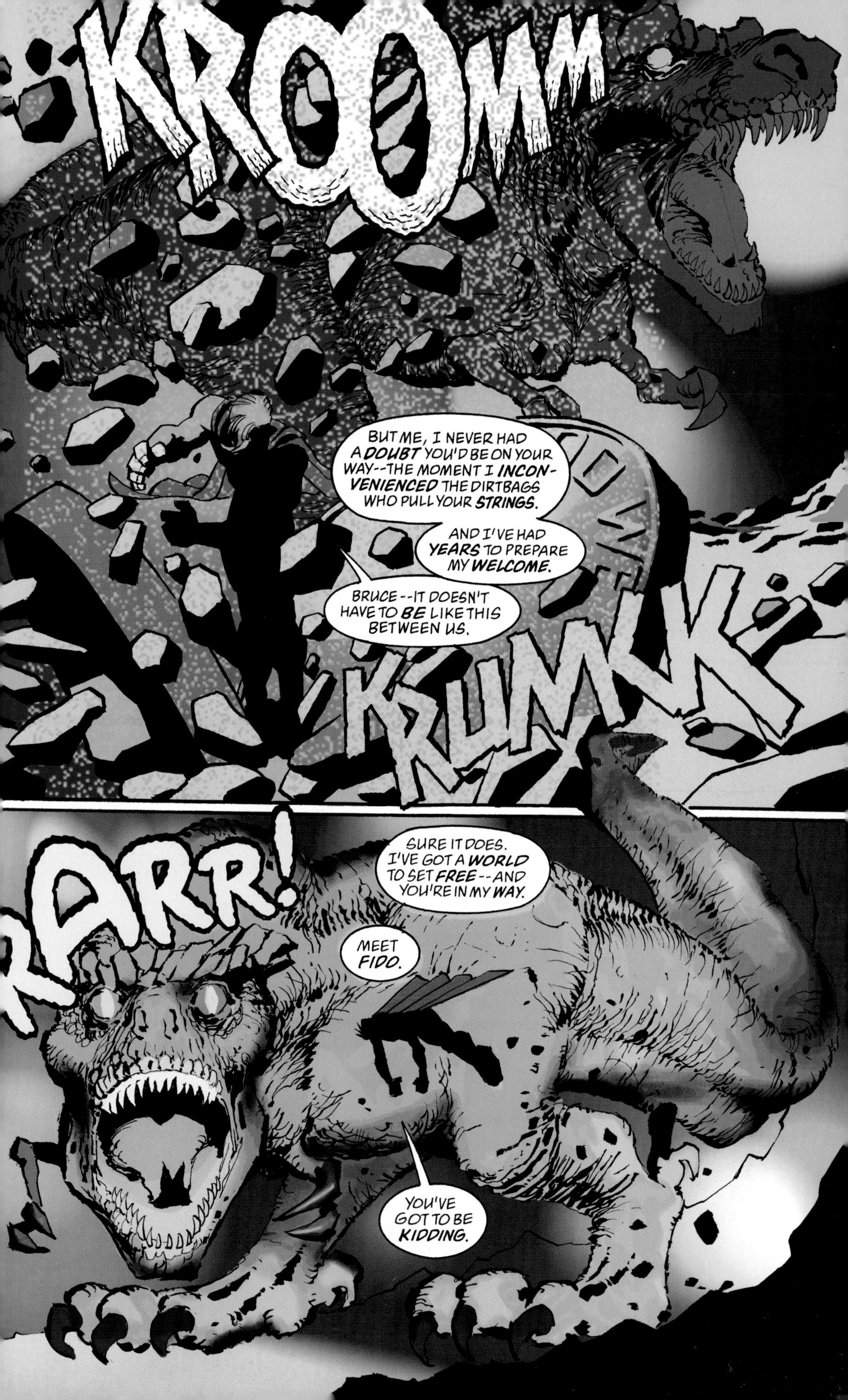
KROOMM
BUT ME, I NEVER HAD A DOUBT YOU'D BE ON YOUR WAY--THE MOMENT I INCONVENIENCED THE DIRTBAGS WHO PULL YOUR STRINGS.
AND I'VE HAD YEARS TO PREPARE MY WELCOME.
BRUCE--IT DOESN'T HAVE TO BE LIKE THIS BETWEEN US.
KRUNK!
SURE IT DOES. I'VE GOT A WORLD TO SET FREE--AND YOU'RE IN MY WAY.
MEET FIDO.
YOU'VE GOT TO BE KIDDING.

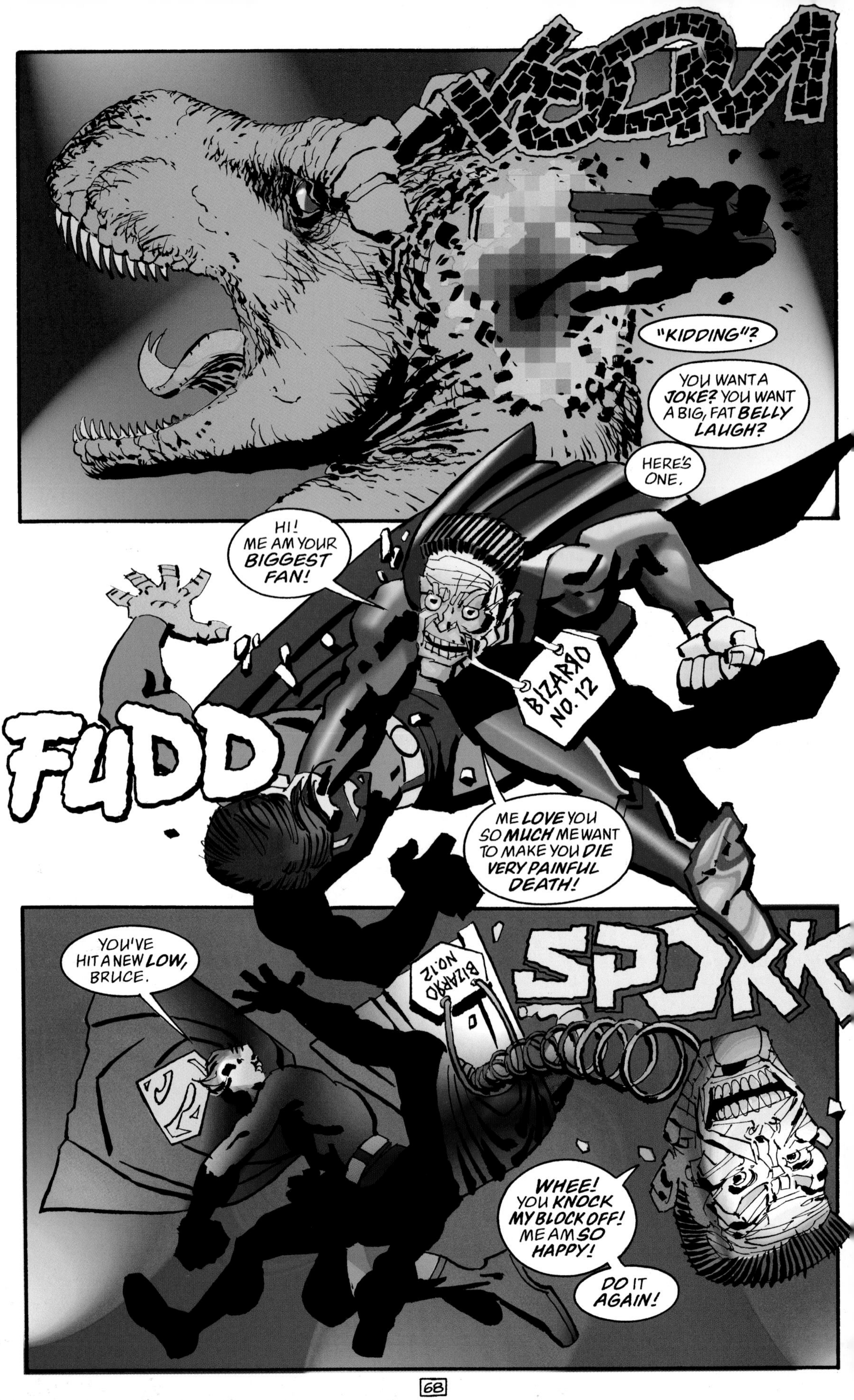
"KIDDING"?
YOU WANT A JOKE? YOU WANT A BIG, FAT BELLY LAUGH?
HERE'S ONE.
HI! ME AM YOUR BIGGEST FAN!
BIZARRO NO. 12
FUDD
ME LOVE YOU SO MUCH ME WANT TO MAKE YOU DIE VERY PAINFUL DEATH!
YOU'VE HIT A NEW LOW, BRUCE.
BIZARRO NO. 12
WHEE! YOU KNOCK MY BLOCK OFF! ME AM SO HAPPY!
DO IT AGAIN!

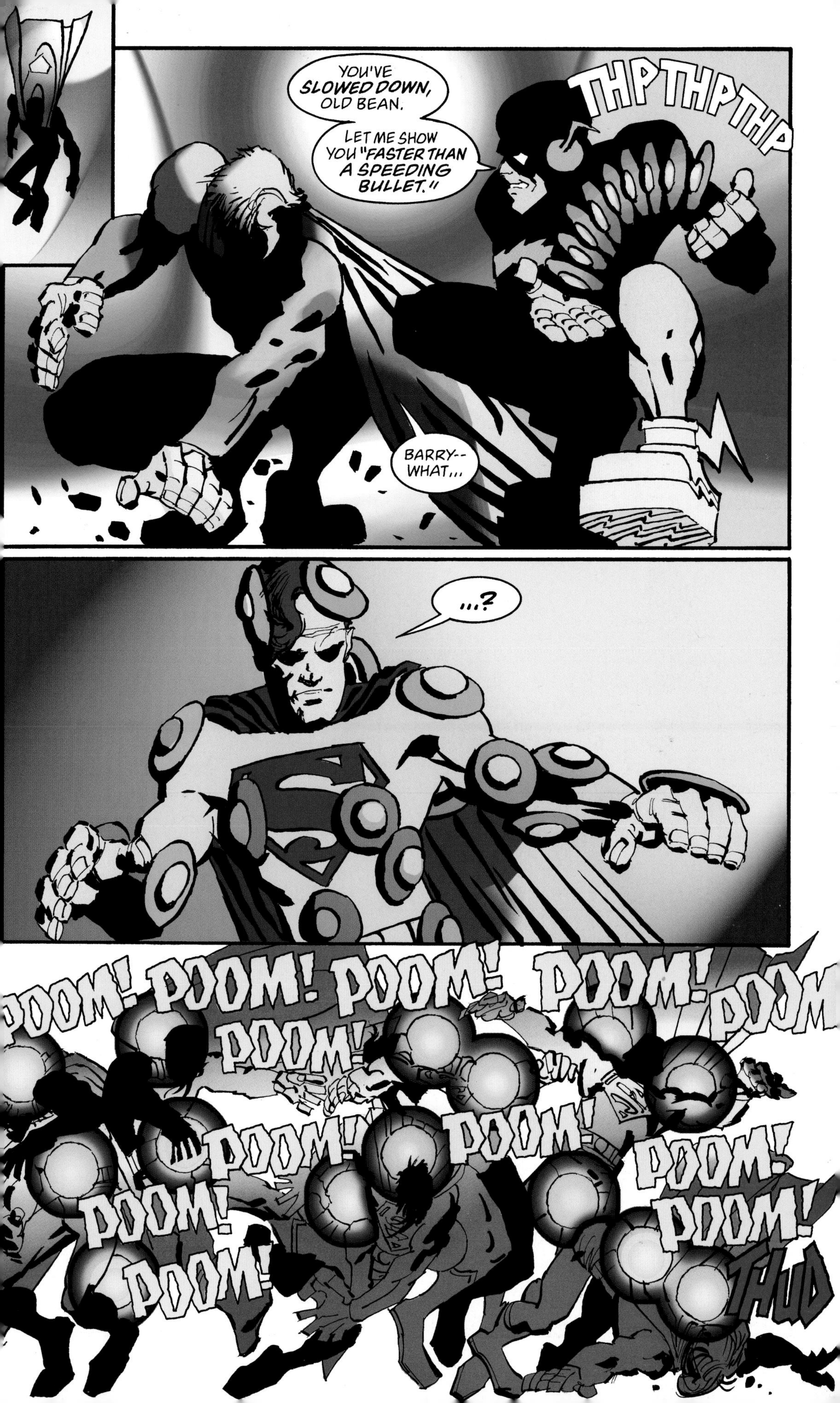
YOU'VE SLOWED DOWN, OLD BEAN.
LET ME SHOW YOU "FASTER THAN A SPEEDING BULLET."
THPTHPTHP
BARRY-- WHAT...
...?
POOM! POOM! POOM! POOM! POOM
POOM!
POOM! POOM! POOM!
POOM!
POOM!
POOM!
POOM!
THUD

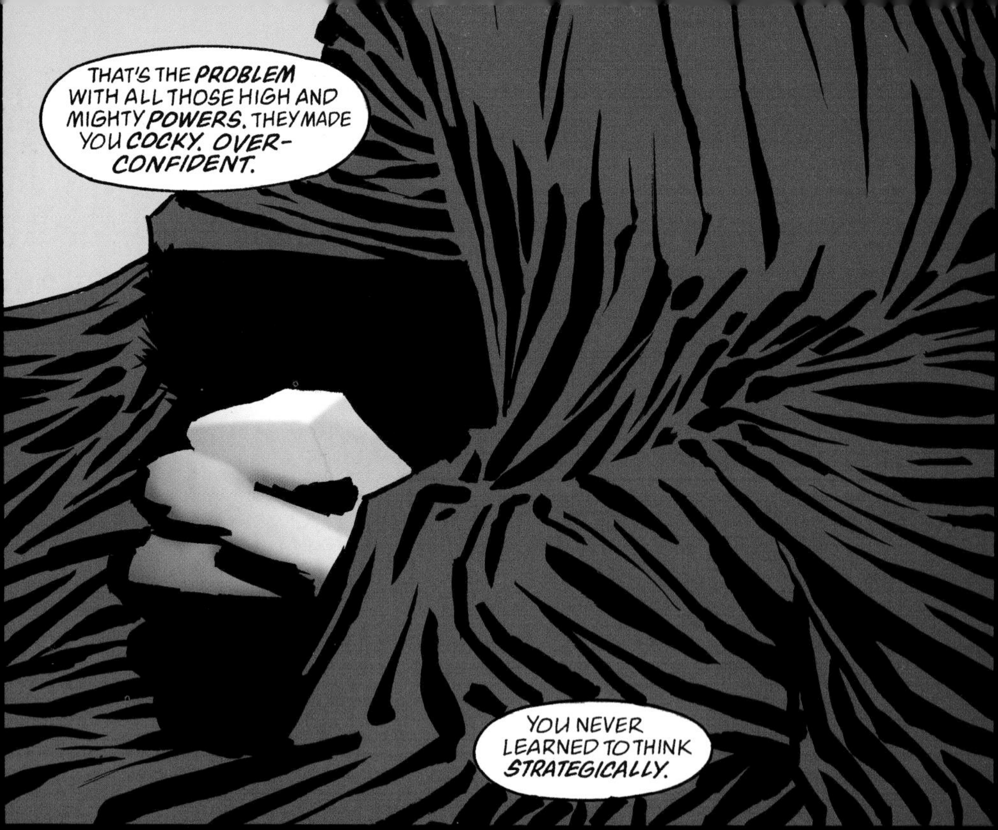

THAT'S THE PROBLEM WITH ALL THOSE HIGH AND MIGHTY POWERS. THEY MADE YOU COCKY. OVER-CONFIDENT.
YOU NEVER LEARNED TO THINK STRATEGICALLY.

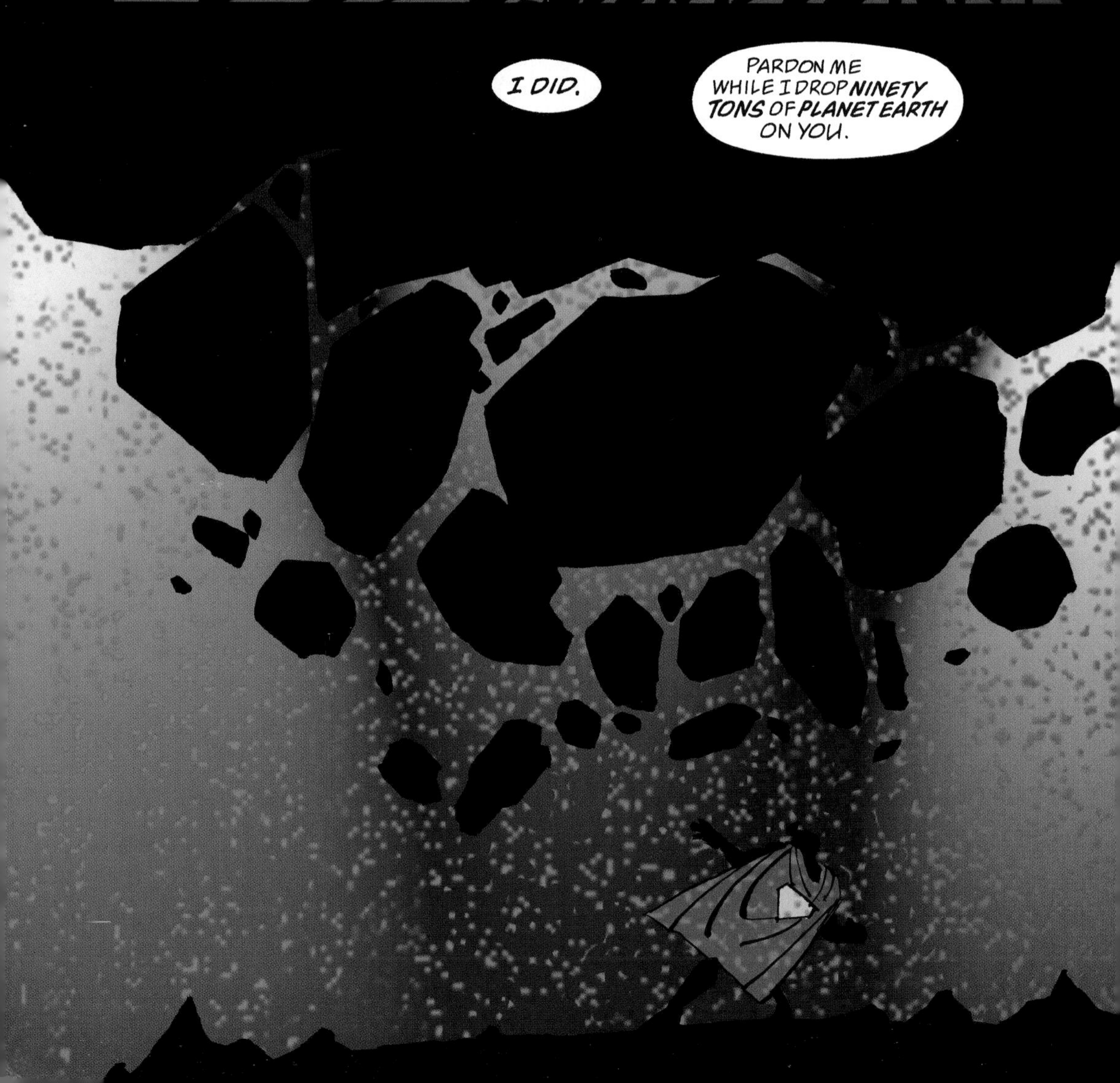

I DID.
PARDON ME WHILE I DROP NINETY TONS OF PLANET EARTH ON YOU.

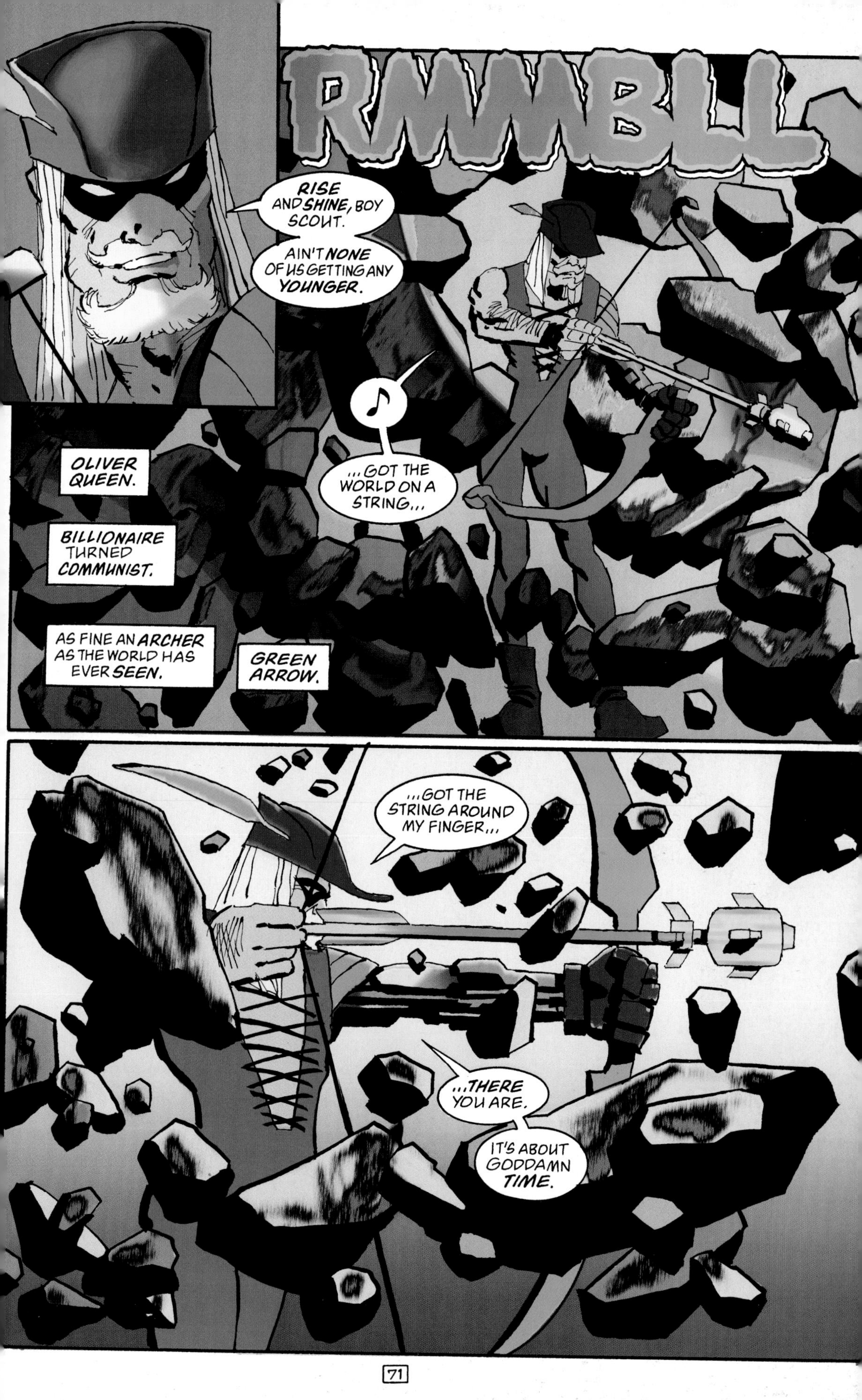
RMMBLL
RISE AND SHINE, BOY SCOUT.
AIN'T NONE OF US GETTING ANY YOUNGER.
♪
...GOT THE WORLD ON A STRING...
OLIVER QUEEN.
BILLIONAIRE TURNED COMMUNIST.
AS FINE AN ARCHER AS THE WORLD HAS EVER SEEN.
GREEN ARROW.
...GOT THE STRING AROUND MY FINGER...
...THERE YOU ARE.
IT'S ABOUT GODDAMN TIME.

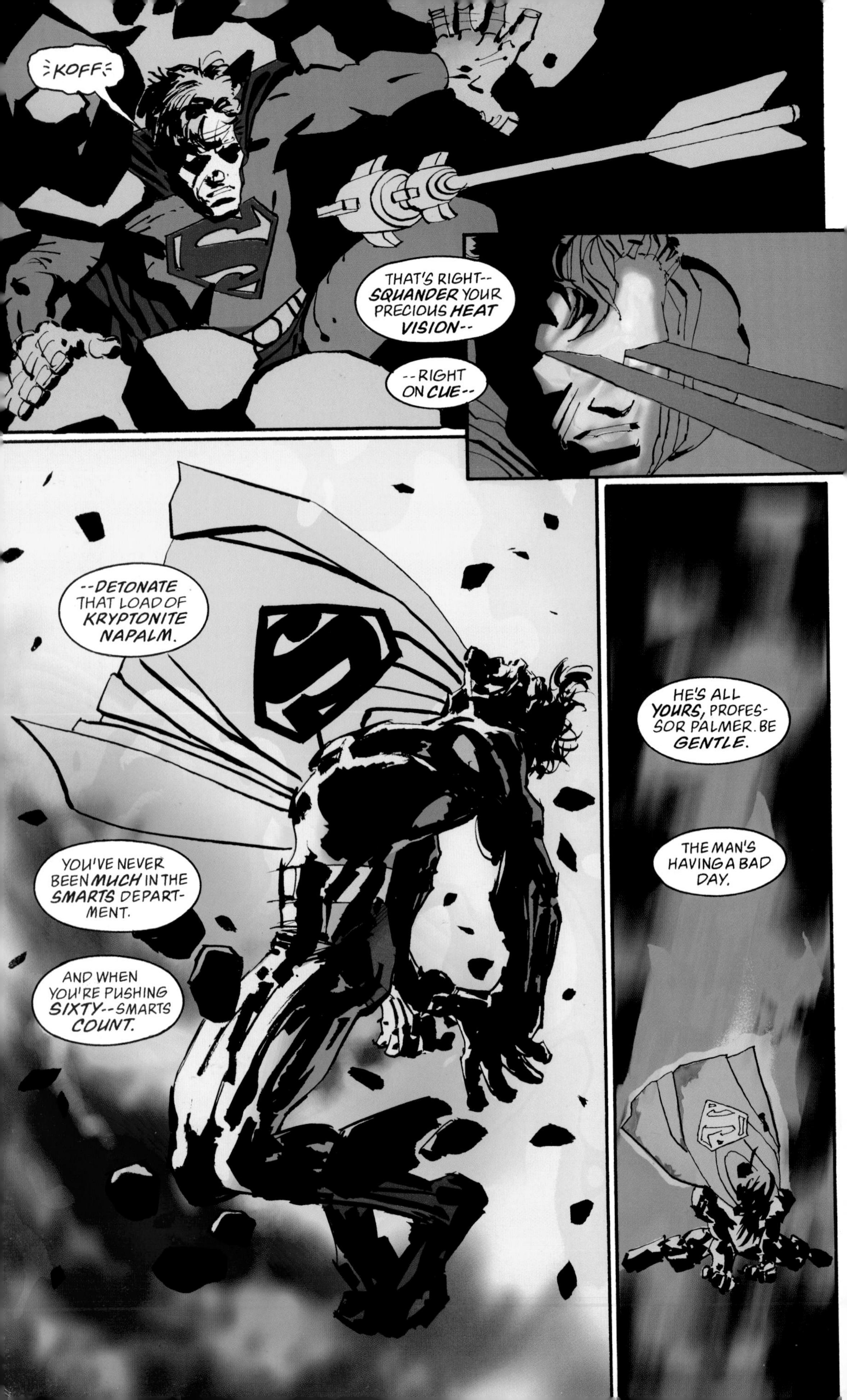
KOFF
THAT'S RIGHT-- SQUANDER YOUR PRECIOUS HEAT VISION--
--RIGHT ON CUE--
--DETONATE THAT LOAD OF KRYPTONITE NAPALM.
YOU'VE NEVER BEEN MUCH IN THE SMARTS DEPARTMENT.
AND WHEN YOU'RE PUSHING SIXTY--SMARTS COUNT.
HE'S ALL YOURS, PROFESSOR PALMER. BE GENTLE.
THE MAN'S HAVING A BAD DAY.

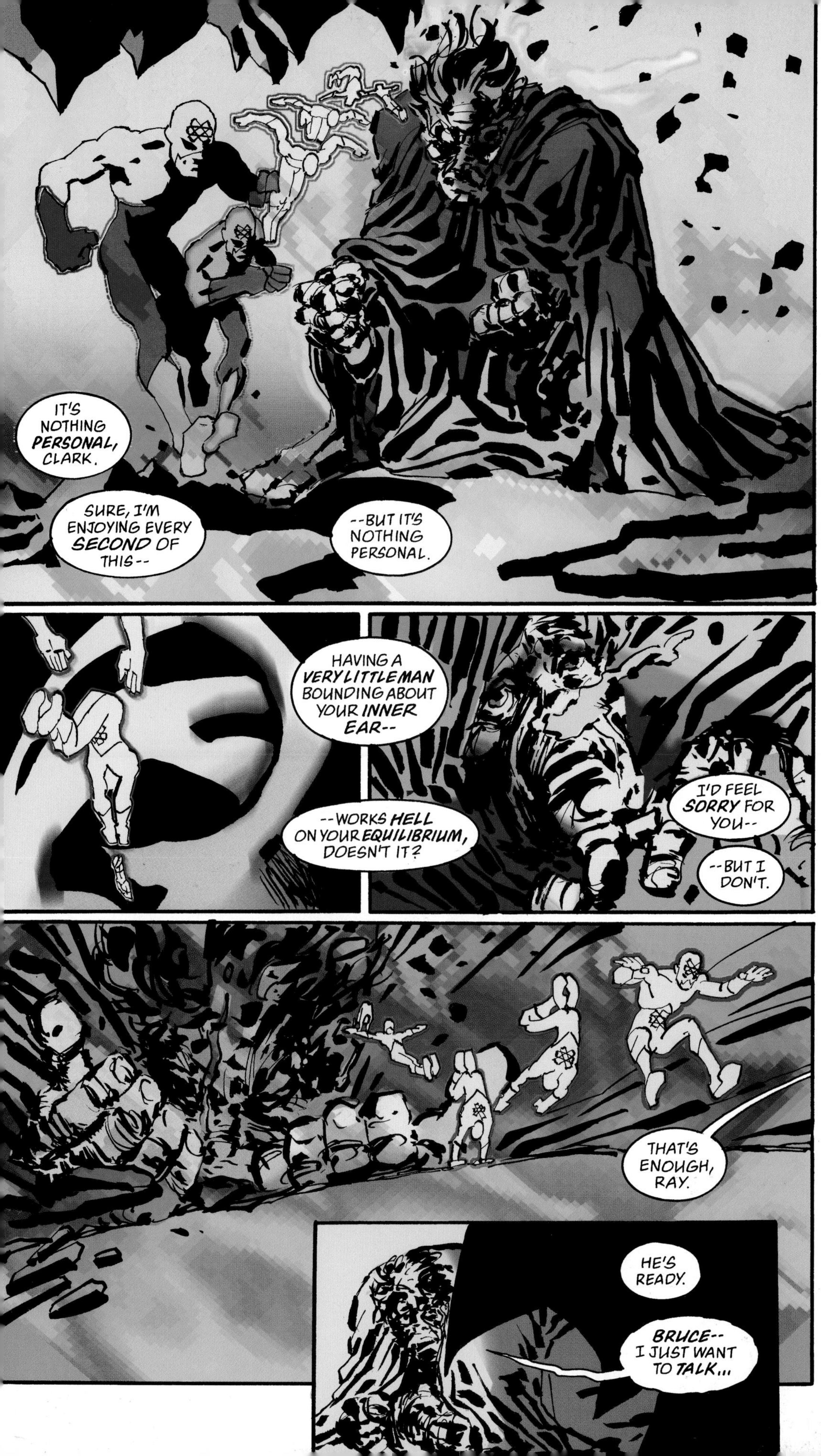

IT'S NOTHING **PERSONAL,** CLARK.
SURE, I'M ENJOYING EVERY **SECOND** OF THIS--
--BUT IT'S NOTHING PERSONAL.
HAVING A **VERY LITTLE MAN** BOUNDING ABOUT YOUR **INNER EAR**--
--WORKS **HELL** ON YOUR **EQUILIBRIUM,** DOESN'T IT?
I'D FEEL **SORRY** FOR YOU--
--BUT I DON'T.
THAT'S ENOUGH, RAY.
HE'S READY.
BRUCE-- I JUST WANT TO **TALK**...

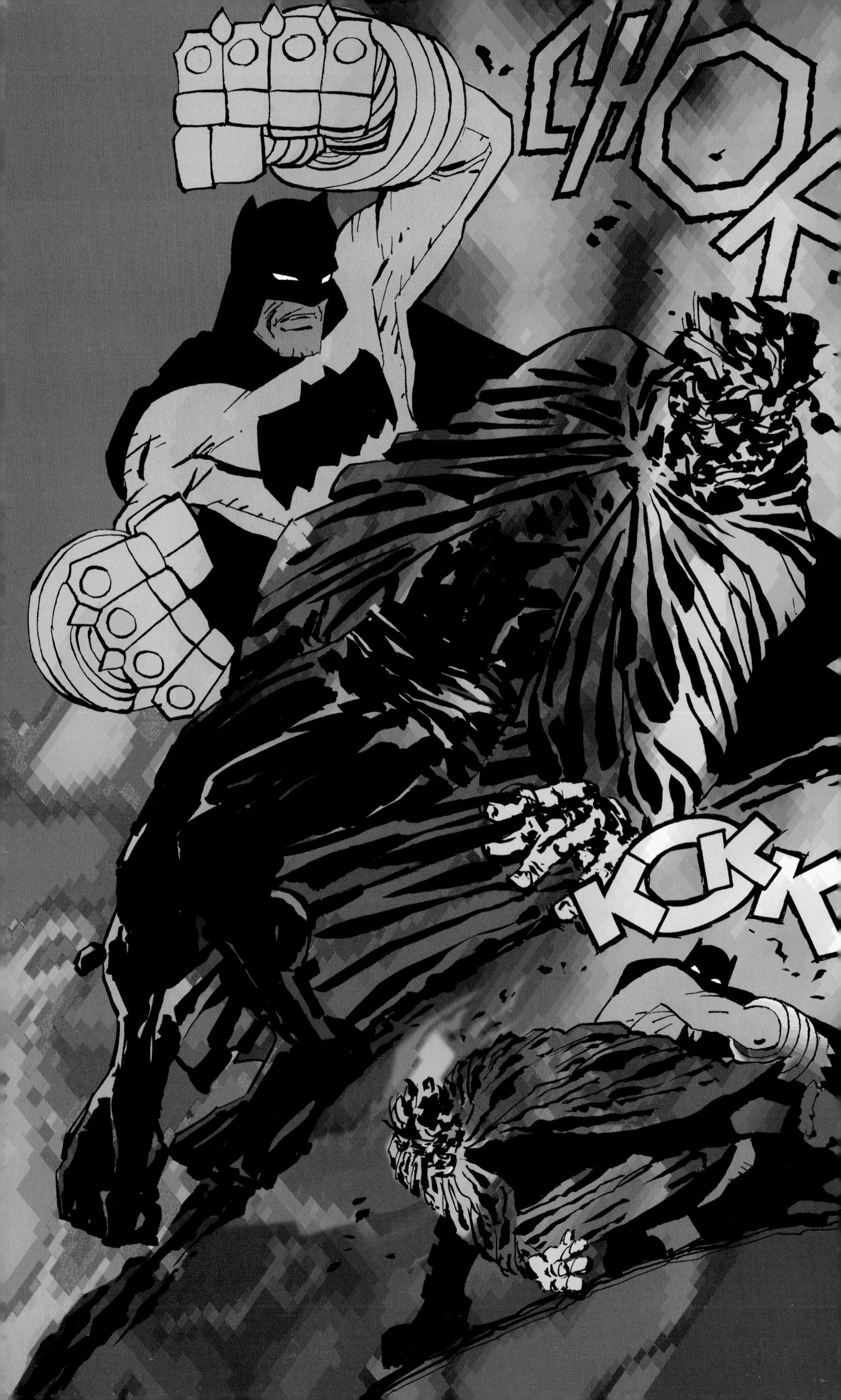
CHOK
KCK

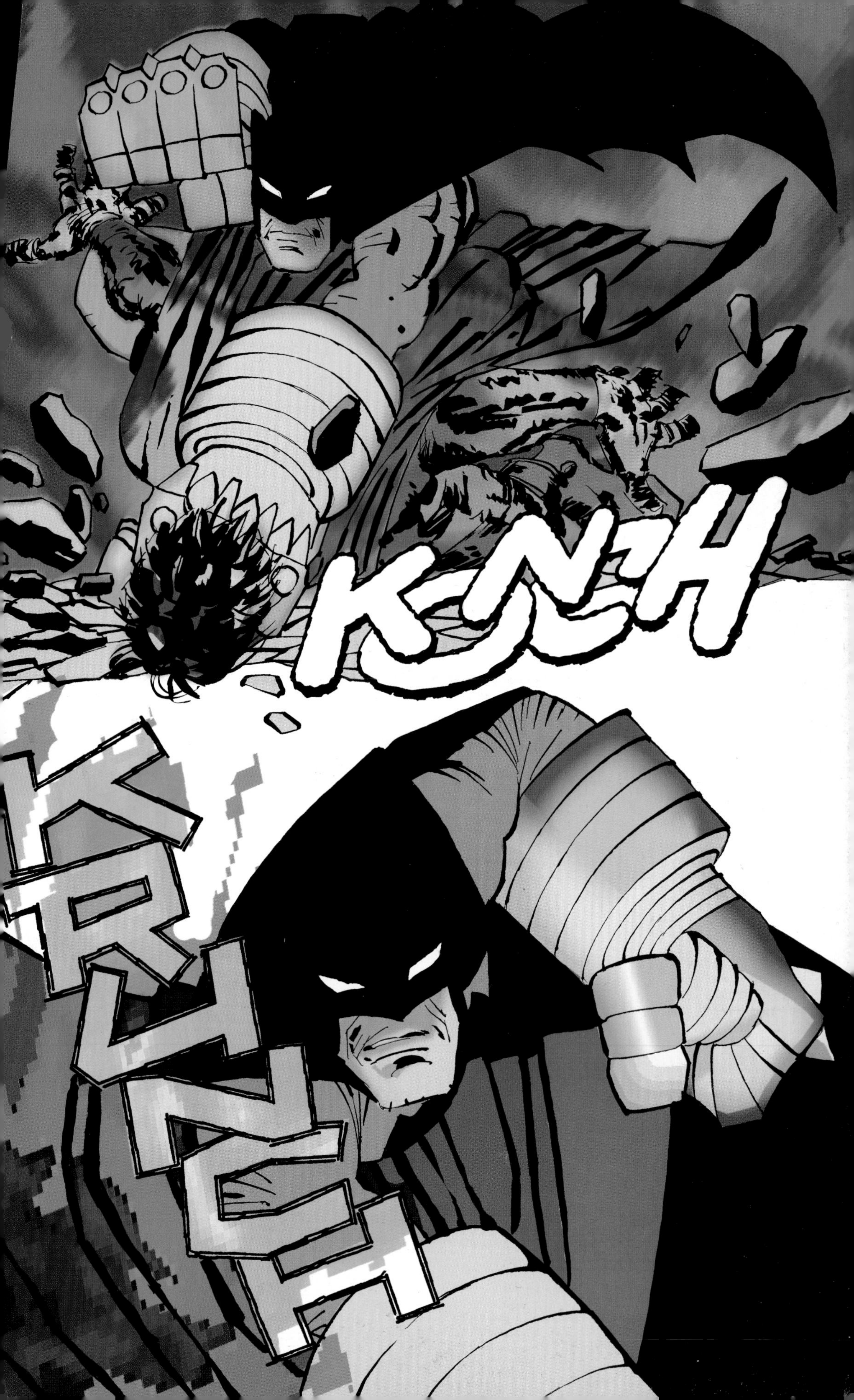
KNCH
KRZZUT

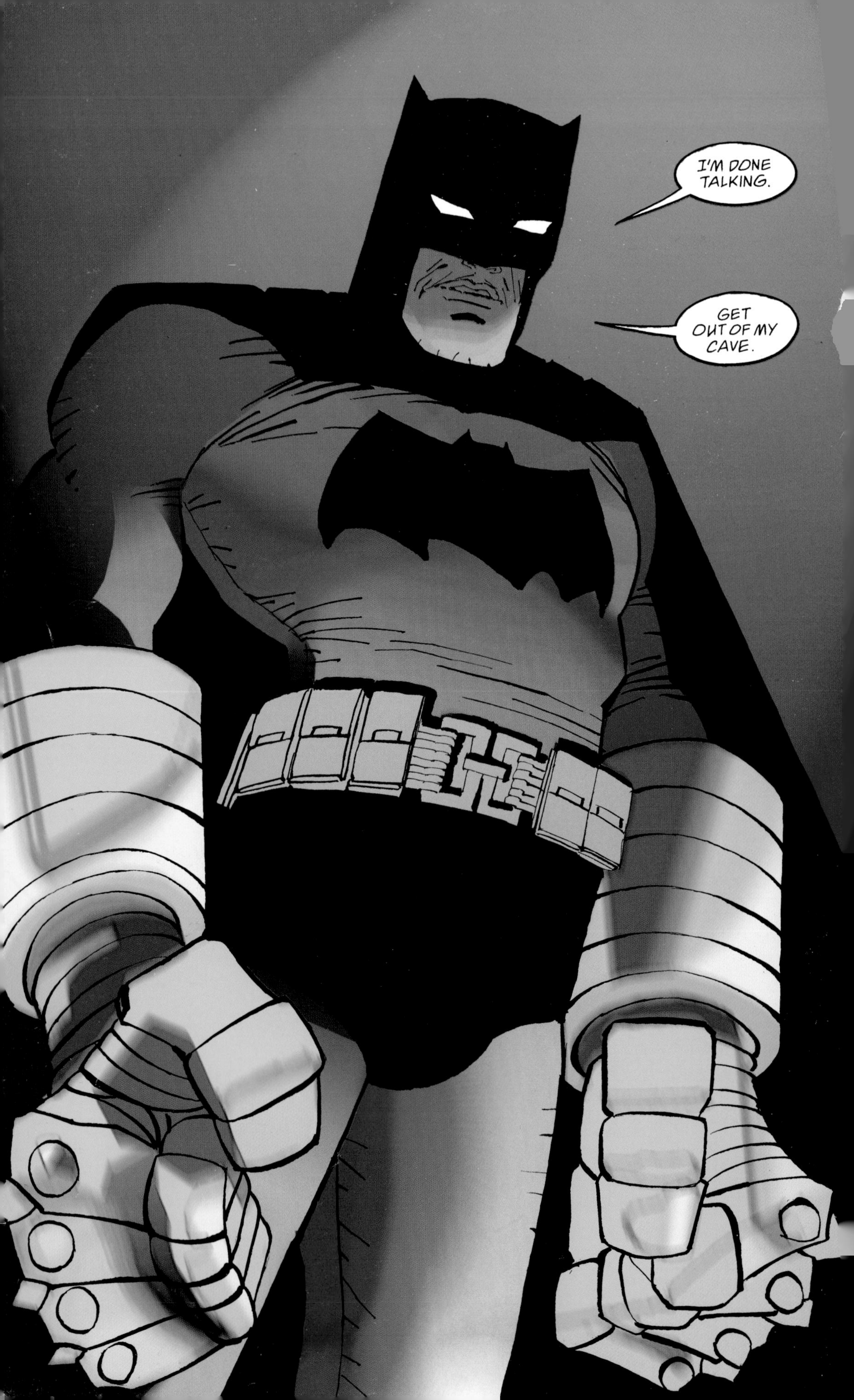
I'M DONE TALKING.
GET OUT OF MY CAVE.